Textiles
of the Arts and Crafts
Movement

LINDA PARRY

Textiles of the Arts and Crafts Movement

with 153 illustrations,
50 in color

THAMES AND HUDSON

For Sarah, Max and Daniel

1. (*frontispiece*) Samuel Rowe: silk and wool double cloth
woven by A. H. Lee & Sons, *c.* 1896.

© 1988 The Board of Trustees of the Victoria and Albert Museum, London
Layout © 1988 Thames and Hudson Ltd, London
Reprinted 1990

First published in the United States in 1988 by
Thames and Hudson Inc., 500 Fifth Avenue,
New York, New York 10110

Library of Congress Catalog Card Number 87-51290

Printed and bound in Spain by Artes Graficas Toledo S.A.
D.L.: TO–415–1990

Contents

Acknowledgments

THE PREPARATION of this book has only been possible through the cooperation of colleagues in the Department of Textile Furnishings and Dress at the Victoria and Albert Museum; my thanks go to each and every one of them. I would particularly like to mention Santina Levey for allowing the project to get off the ground, Natalie Rothstein for spending many hours reading my text and offering advice, Debbie Sinfield for listing and typing and Alyson Morris for helping prepare items for photography. Hilary Young of the Department of Designs, Prints and Drawings has been very helpful and Daniel McGrath has taken most of the beautiful photographs. My especial gratitude goes to Neil Harvey without whose excellent assistance I could not have written the book in so short a time.

Colleagues in Europe and America have been very helpful to me over the past two years and, whereas my work abroad concerned a wider based research project, I would like to take this opportunity to offer them all my heartfelt thanks. For providing information and illustrations for this book I am particularly grateful to Astri Aasen of Trondheim, Dr Sigrid Barden of Zurich, Ursula Strate of Hamburg, Carol J. Callahan of the Glessner House, Chicago, Gillian Moss of the Cooper-Hewitt Museum, New York, Charlotte Paludan of Copenhagen, Dr Heike Schroder of Stuttgart, Brigitte Tiezel of Krefeld, and Ann Wardwell of Cleveland, Ohio.

Norah Gillow of the William Morris Gallery, Walthamstow, Dr Jennifer Harris and Maud Wallace of the Whitworth Art Gallery, Manchester, Elizabeth Arthur of Glasgow City Museum and Art Gallery, Mr J. Rogers of Liverpool City Libraries and David Chandler of the National Portrait Gallery have also been of assistance. I have been grateful for the opportunity to study at the Public Record Office, National Monuments Record, Westminster Public Libraries, the Silver Studio Collection at Middlesex Polytechnic and the National Art Library Archive, of which I would like to thank the staff, especially Meg Sweet and Eva White. A number of textile firms have allowed me to study their historic collection and I am indebted to Ann Lynch and Audrey Duck of G. P. & J. Baker and Bernadine Gregory of Courtaulds.

Finally I would like to acknowledge the help and encouragement of a number of individuals: Andrew Cox, A. R. Dufty, Christopher Harrison, James and Lucilla Joll, Stephen Lee, the late Jocelyn Morton, Mrs June Randall, Paul and Siobhan Reeves, Margaret Swain, Mark Turner, Jean Wells, Michael Whiteway, and Christine Woods. I owe a special form of gratitude to my family and friends whose patience and forbearance has often gone far beyond the call of duty.

LINDA PARRY
January 1988

Preface

I HAVE never been happy to use the expression 'Arts and Crafts' as a descriptive term as there is no one historic style that matches such an all-embracing yet nebulous title. Despite this, it has been over the years applied to most forms of British and American decorative art produced between 1880 and 1920, irrespective of origin, design or manufacture. Unifying factors do exist, however, and no alternative expression has been found that would do as well, despite the words having little meaning in themselves.

This book concentrates on one particular craft, textiles, which, through the efforts of the individuals involved, was for a short period elevated to a higher art form because of its popularity throughout the fashionable centres of the world and because of its influence on manufacture, which has lasted since that time. To explain that phenomenon, this study concentrates on the individuals involved and work shown in London by the Arts and Crafts Exhibition Society. The importance of the Society cannot be overestimated: it not only provided a name for the Movement but gave a group of artists and designers a chance to display their work in socially and artistically sympathetic surroundings.

The formation of the Arts and Crafts Exhibition Society and the opening of the first exhibition were recorded by participants, and accounts have appeared since then offering different interpretations of their aims. While I have tried to present a full and accurate picture as a fitting celebration of the Society's centenary, my study is limited to a single art, textiles, and is confined to work exhibited between 1888, when the first exhibition was held, and 1916. All aspects of textile manufacture are included as they appeared in the various exhibitions with hand-made tapestries, carpets and embroideries alongside commercially produced woven and printed fabrics. The finest collection of these textiles and the designs for them belongs to the Victoria and Albert Museum in London, although there are important pieces in other collections.

To conclude this study in 1916 might seem somewhat arbitrary but that date marks the end of the period because of changing styles and techniques. It is also significant as the exhibition for that year was held at the Royal Academy, the institution whose prohibitive display policy had forced the setting up of the Society in 1888. It was the last exhibition before the catastrophic effects of the Great War were felt, while the Omega Workshop had already produced its first textiles with purely abstract designs. Plain handloom weaving had become one of the most popular craft techniques together with hand block-printing. The commercial textile industry, unable to produce such effects, and lacking the confidence which had been such an important factor in earlier success, turned away from encouraging individual skills and original designs to the reproduction of historic patterns. All this was

2. Tailpiece used in the Arts and Crafts Exhibition catalogues.

done in an attempt to compete in the fashionable interior design market in which eclecticism now prevailed. Similarly, May Morris and Grace Christie advocated a return to traditional skills in embroidery despite the new order of experimental work influencing the teaching of needlework in schools. The First World War proved to be the turning point and never again did industrial and craft work have the unity of production and design or the comradeship of spirit experienced in the preceding twenty years. One of the most original artistic movements seen for centuries had come to an end.

The Catalogue on pp.117-53 lists the main designers, craftsmen, institutions and firms involved in textile production during this period. Literally hundreds of individuals took some part in the production of textiles displayed at the exhibitions, whether as designer, weaver, printer, embroiderer, manufacturer or retailer. Although it is impossible to list them all (one of the most important rules of the exhibitions), it is hoped that by a closer study of their textiles the aims and ramifications of the Movement can be fully appreciated.

3. Walter Crane: ornament from an early Arts and Crafts Exhibition Society leaflet.

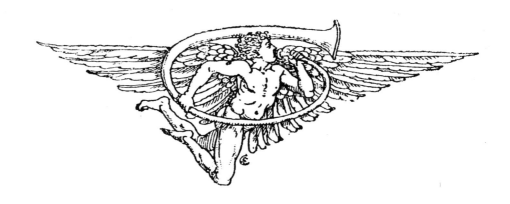

Introduction

THROUGHOUT the latter part of the nineteenth century efforts were made to reform the Royal Academy, which had become an institution of privilege and limited scope. From 1886, this subject became one of the main discussion points in the art press, where certain revisions to the rules of the Academy were advocated in an attempt to bring democracy to the hallowed steps of Burlington House. As well as limiting the number of works submitted by each contributor (to two, with four for each Academician, was suggested) journalists and correspondents alike believed that a fairer election of members would be gained by offering all exhibitors equal suffrage and that elected membership of the Council and the Hanging and Selection Committees should be for a fixed term only. Their aim was to break the stranglehold of a small clique of leading artists and to restore the scope of the Academy's exhibitions beyond the easel paintings which dominated every show. Furthermore, the Academy had, for a number of years, reneged on its duties towards education.[1] Holman Hunt in an article, 'The Reform of the Royal Academy' (*The British Architect*, 27 August 1886), called for a revision of the Academy's attitude towards teaching, to 'render needless the exodus of students to Paris'.

The art press, always at variance with the Academy because of the high-handed and shoddy treatment it had experienced at its hands,[2] was keen to show the strong feelings of the art world towards revision. The *Art Journal* conducted a survey of exhibiting oil painters resulting in 273 in favour and only 6 against general reforms (they were at pains to point out, in their report of March 1886, that two of the latter were women), and *The British Architect* for 3 September 1886 further stressed the unfairness of the Academy's attitude towards all the arts except painting. This show of teeth by the architectural fraternity, in particular, led to such drastic outside reform that within ten years the attention of practising artists and the general public had been so forcefully turned away from the Academy that it never regained its prestigious place as the ultimate exhibiting institution for the arts in Britain.

For a number of years the Academy had failed to represent architecture adequately in its exhibitions. In 1886 there were fifty-nine painters and only five architects among the Academicians (seven sculptors and two engravers completed the numbers), and there had been no attempt to appoint a Professor of Architecture since the death of G. E. Street in 1881. From the second quarter of the nineteenth century architects, following the lead of A. W. N. Pugin, had become more involved in all aspects of the arts, concerning themselves not only with the decoration and furnishing of their own buildings but also with free-lance design for all branches of the decorative arts. It is likely that this new more rounded attitude had a direct bearing on the views of the Academy which relegated architecture to the 'Lesser' or 'Applied Arts' and as such no longer its concern.

Loss of confidence in the Royal Academy had been felt for some years before the evidence of unrest was shown in the press of 1886. With no unifying body, opposition took the form of a number of small groups set up by disenchanted architects, painters, sculptors and designers who met in an effort to discuss their work and art in general. Even at this early stage, the prevailing attitude at these meetings quickly changed from one of iconoclasm to enthusiasm for a new future, a mood encouraged by a more rational attitude towards art and life as advocated in the writings of John Ruskin (in particular his chapter 'The Nature of Gothic' in the second volume of *The Stones of Venice*, published in 1853) and by William Morris in his published works and through the evidence of his own workshop. The prevailing optimism of the times set the tone for the movement that followed and greatly contributed to its style and subsequent success.

Two of these groups, one comprising architects and the other more general designers, proved particularly significant. The 'St George's Art Society' was formed by pupils and apprentices of the architect Richard Norman Shaw[3] and took its name from a church in Bloomsbury. Set up in 1883 in opposition to both the Royal Academy and the Institute of British Architects, the group hoped to recruit members 'who were neither the oil painters of the Academy nor the Surveyors of the Institute, but craftsmen in architecture, painting, sculpture and the kindred arts'.[4] The other group, 'The Fifteen', first met in 1881 at the instigation of Lewis F. Day, the decorative arts designer and art critic, and included Walter Crane, Henry Holiday, T. M. Rooke, J. D. Sedding and Hugh Stannus amongst its members.[5] The name was derived from a popular puzzle ('some trick with fifteen numbers and one blank in a square box'[6]) and an amusing drawing of the symbol incorporates caricatures of the founding members, coincidentally also fifteen. They met at members' houses once a month from October to May 'to discuss subjects of common interest to themselves and bearing upon various branches of design'.[7] As some of the Fifteen produced designs for textiles they are of particular interest but the only existing information concerns work done individually outside the group.

In 1884 the Art Workers' Guild was formed. As the leading members of this new organization were taken from the two smaller clubs, it has always been seen as the direct result of their amalgamation, although this is a simplification. However, it obviously met with the approval of both groups as each was subsequently absorbed by it. The Guild was set up specifically as a forum and meeting place for practising artists and designers, and its social benefits are appreciated to this day. 'It is not a school, it is not a Club, it is not a Debating Society. In the A.-W. G. I find something of the spirit of the Studio life of Rome', wrote the Guild's first master, the sculptor George Blackall Simonds, in 1885.[8] However, this 'Studio' was neither an exhibition centre nor a revision parlour for the arts and despite acceptance by all that the fine and applied arts were worthy of equal artistic endeavour, there was still no means for members to prove this point publicly or to advertise their own work.

In the wake of an inevitable refusal by the Royal Academy to reform, a letter signed by Holman Hunt, Walter Crane and George Clausen was sent to the news and art press and published in a number of papers including *The Times* on the morning of 7 August

1886.[9] Describing the Academy as 'a private society' they stated, rather sarcastically, that it 'should be left to enjoy its rights in peace'. The signatories went on to suggest that instead of trying to force small reforms, the public would be best served with the 'establishment of a really national exhibition, which should be conducted by artists on the broadest and fairest lines – in which no artist should have rights of place; and all works should be chosen by a jury elected by and from all artists in the kingdom.'[10]

4. Walter Crane: detail of the symbol of the Fifteen, with caricatures of the Secretary, Lewis F. Day, in a chariot, and Crane himself, riding a crane.

The letter had dramatic and far-reaching effects, galvanizing the art world into direct and positive action after years of apathy. Within a short time a printed sheet entitled 'National Exhibition for the Arts', signed by more than four hundred of the country's leading artists and designers, was circulated, inviting membership of 'an artistic co-operative society in which all who join will have a distinct voice in its management'.[11] Lively interest was shown in the new movement and press reports were accompanied by letters of support. In 1887 the organization was established. Documents concerning the first meetings[12] show proposals that it should comprise five sections covering architecture, the applied arts, painting, sculpture and engraving, and that each should have equal representation on the Committee. Official recognition of the equality of all the practical arts was long overdue, but not simply because of the intransigence of historic precedent and the prevailing hierarchical attitude of the Royal Academy. With the popularity of Japanese art in Britain from the 1860s the Eastern attitude, in which no barriers between the various branches of the arts were perceived, had become widely adopted in artistic circles and was now both fashionable and sensible in an increasingly commercial world.

It was not long before plans to hold a national exhibition ran into trouble. At the Committee's meeting in February 1887 George Clausen, with the support of other artists of the New English Art Club, proposed that 'an effort should be made to secure the equal suffrage of the Artists in the Exhibition of the Royal Academy'. Somewhat exasperated with this continued pandering to the Academy, Walter Crane proposed an amendment, recorded as follows: 'That in consideration of the aims of the movement which the present Provisional Committee represent are larger than any reform of the Royal Academy will cover. It is desirable to work on independant lines to attain our object.'[13] With this statement Crane sealed his fate and that of a few of his colleagues. Clausen's proposal was accepted and they resigned.[14]

This action can be seen as the true beginning of the Arts and Crafts Exhibition Society and the subsequent Movement to which it gave its name, although claims of authorship were made by both W. A. S. Benson and A. H. Mackmurdo. Mackmurdo believed that the Society was a direct development of his own Century Guild set up in 1882 'to render all branches of art the sphere no longer of the tradesman but of the artist'.[15] Whereas the artists of the Arts and Crafts Movement also believed that an improvement in the standard of design would come from the designer and not the trader, they saw this improvement developing from the harmonious relationship of craftsmen and designers (often the same) of like artistic views. Objects designed under the Guild's name, furniture and textiles for instance, were manufactured by commercial firms, the designers having little involvement in their manufacture. It is in this important point that the two organizations differed.

The proof of Benson's claim is far more tangible, being two scribbled notes to his neighbour (probably Heywood Sumner) at the fateful meeting of the National Exhibition

5

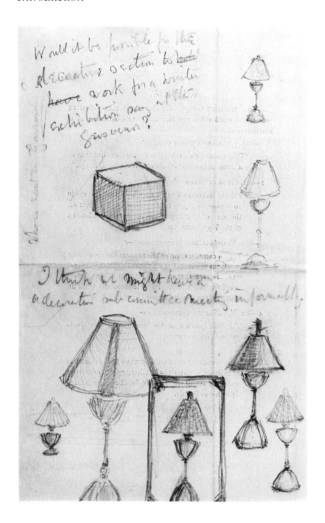

5. W. A. S. Benson's notes, on the back of a printed programme, in which he suggests an exhibition of decorative arts.

6. Walter Crane, photographed by Frederick Hollyer in 1886.

for the Arts at which Clausen's proposal was read. In these notes Benson asked 'Would it be possible for the decorative section to work for a winter exhibition say at the Grosvenor?' and added 'I think we might have a decoration sub committee meeting informally'.[16]

Ironically, important events often have such humble beginnings but in reality most individual aspirations only come to fruition through much collective effort. In March 1887 seven artists and designers (Benson, Crane, Day, Heywood Sumner, Henry Longden, Mervyn Macartney and J. Hungerford Pollen) met at the metalworker Longden's house in order to draw up a letter inviting artists and craftsmen to form the nucleus of an association 'for securing an Exhibition of the Combined Arts'. Of the twenty-five people contacted sixteen replied positively and the first meeting of the Provisional Committee was held at the Charing Cross Hotel on 11 May 1887. At this meeting Crane was elected Chairman and Benson agreed to act as Secretary and temporary Honorary Treasurer. The experience of several false starts by other organizations led the Committee to write immediately to Sir Coutts Lindsay requesting the use of the Grosvenor Gallery, then the most fashionable venue in London, for their first exhibition. At the second meeting on 25 May, the

7. Walter Crane: original ink design for the letterhead of the Arts and Crafts Exhibition Society.

bookbinder T. J. Cobden-Sanderson proposed that the name 'Arts and Crafts Exhibition Society' should be adopted and the motion was seconded by Lewis F. Day. With a new identity and plans for the first exhibition the Society had achieved more in three months than had been possible in the preceding four years.

The Arts and Crafts Exhibition Society did not provide either the first ideas or the first opportunity for the display of decorative arts in nineteenth-century Britain. The International Exhibitions of 1851 and 1862 and the shows which followed set up by the Royal Society of Arts had all concentrated on this aspect of the arts. However, as trade fairs, and as a means of advertising British manufacture, they concentrated on technical innovation rather than original design, for it was in this sphere that foreign investment was most easily attracted and British industry had the best chance for expansion. Manufacturers were consequently listed in the catalogues and received the various prizes but few individual designers or craftsmen were mentioned.

The effect on the working man of the mechanical free-for-all, which demanded centralization of manufacture and created both great wealth and great poverty, was well documented in the literature of the day and led to much needed social reform. With a less exclusive approach to art and the consequent broadening of their design activities, artists became aware of the conditions in the industries for which they designed and many found these conditions not to their taste. William Morris, alerted to them by Ruskin, criticized a system that allowed British craftsmen to lose both their skills and their self-respect while at the same time industry became rich by manufacturing technically brilliant yet artistically dead products. In his publications, in his lectures and in his own work he attempted to redress the balance by improving the standard of design and restoring pleasure and self-respect to the worker. The revival of traditional techniques, including vegetable dyeing and the block-printing of textiles, at his own factory enabled him to achieve an aesthetically pleasing balance between the craft (technique) and art (the decoration) and a public ready for a new look in their shops saw what could be achieved.

Although modern misconceptions deny it, Morris and his contemporaries were not opposed to all forms of mechanization. To facilitate textile production Morris would have used steam-driven jacquard looms if he could have afforded to install them. Lewis F. Day in his book *Everyday Art* (1882) suggested that machinery, steam power, and 'electricity for all we know' were likely to have an effect on future design. Both men, however, despite differing political views, firmly believed that its use in industry required careful consideration.

While the example of workshops producing a number of artistic products under one roof was to be emulated some years later by a few rural groups, the scope of Morris & Co. was never equalled and it can be said that the industrial and artistic world benefited more from Morris's views than from his actual designs.

Recent critics have tried to minimize the influence of William Morris. Yet writing in 1902, just six years after Morris's death, J. Scarratt Rigby, himself a successful designer, described Morris's profound effect on contemporary decorative arts.[17]

> Some of these arts almost owe their existence to the prodigious mental force and untiring vigour he brought to bear upon them; in others his work, if examined and compared with that of today, will be seen to be the direct parent of some important phases; while many which even his enormous capacity was unable to cope with have received inspiration directly from him or from the group of men of whom he was the acknowledged centre of radiation.

A yearning to return to the traditional skills of the land saw a renewal of interest in the countryside, abandoned by many in the search for employment. Charles Godfrey Leland, an American writer, suggested in his book *Minor Arts* (1880) the formation of classes in rural districts 'for the teaching of simple arts and crafts';[18] and rural classes were indeed soon established. In 1884 the various regional groups were consolidated under the Home Arts and Industries Association (Leland was a Committee member) by a Mrs Jebb with the modest aim 'to teach the minor arts to the working classes thus spreading a knowledge of artistic handiwork among the people'.[19] Annual exhibitions were organized at the Albert Hall and membership automatically guaranteed a display space with each class having its own stall. Work was sold and certificates of merit and medals awarded. Although amateurish in its organization and in much of the work produced, the Association deserves more attention than it has hitherto received. By 1886, schools or classes had been established in fifty-four areas. 'The interest of manufacturers will only be better served by the promotion of sound knowledge and practical skills in the homes of our working classes', wrote *The British Architect* for 25 June 1886, indicating not only an artistic but a sociological interest in the exhibitions and work shown – factors which had become intertwined in the new reforms. Because of the similarity between the views of this organization and those of the later Arts and Crafts Exhibition Society, and the development of a number of the classes into regular Arts and Crafts exhibitors, a description of its working methods can only help to further our knowledge of the later Movement. In an article on the 1905 Albert Hall exhibition the *Art Workers' Quarterly* published the following report:

> The classes commence usually by purely voluntary effort on the part of those who have the welfare of country dwellers or working people at heart. Classes are held in the homes of these voluntary teachers, or in rooms lent by those interested in the work. As the pupils become proficient, professional teaching is engaged, and perhaps work is executed in response to local orders. The class may in time develop into an industry doing work sufficiently well to attract regular custom and thus become self supporting.

Many of these classes developed into commercial concerns and the influence of the Home Arts and Industries Association increased. A review in 1899 expressed delight that what had been 'a small and unnoticed exhibition, should have grown into one so important as to become one of the events of the London season',[20] and early twentieth-century shows were praised in particular for the high standard of embroidery.

The Grosvenor Gallery was not available after all for the first exhibition of the Arts and Crafts Exhibition Society in 1888 and other venues were considered, including the Albert Hall and Waterloo House. The New Gallery in Regent Street, described by Benson as 'then a derelict provision market, afterwards so skillfully converted',[21] was finally chosen for an Autumn exhibition and the £1 collected from each member (originally to meet the Committee's expenses) was further supplemented by larger sums from individuals[22] to meet the costs that would be incurred. The Directors of the New Gallery were offered £300 with a bonus contingent on the success of the first exhibition[23] and a tenancy agreement was signed on 17 September 1888. Ernest Radford was appointed Secretary of the Society at an annual salary of £150 and Finance, Literary and Selection Committees were all formed.

The business-like manner in which the proceedings were organized, with evening lectures and a printed catalogue, must have surprised many onlookers but helped secure what was considered to be a successful venture. Despite such hard work, the members did not lose sight of their original aims in organizing the Society. A. H. Mackmurdo set out these aims in his unpublished memoirs some years later;[24] and although wordy and over flowery, this document provides an invaluable guide to the Movement as an ideological and practical exercise, being written by an artist who was personally involved:

1. To show the British public what could be done by their contemporary fellow craftsmen in making beautiful things for the homes of simple and gentle folk.
2. To revive the desire for beauty in the things of everyday use and to educate the public taste to a preference for art born of one's own day and in one's own country, by periodic exhibitions of standard examples.
3. To arouse among art workers an emulation to excel by placing the work of various craftsmen and designers side by side.
4. To turn industry in the direction of producing such kind of decorative form and ornament as can be produced without detriment by mechanical processes.
5. To raise the status of both craftsman and designer by such publication of authorship as is customary in the fine arts.
6. To give the public some elementary knowledge of, and an intelligent interest in, the processes which determine a thing's formative and decorative character; so that it will look for and esteem those materials and methods which are appropriate to the process of manufacture. This object would be gained by lectures upon principles underlying various types of techniques.

Colour plates

8. Lindsay P. Butterfield: 'Tiger Lily', watercolour design for a printed textile manufactured by G. P. & J. Baker in 1896. The fabric was sold through Heal's from 1898 to 1903 (see Ill. 123).

9. George C. Haité: 'Picotee', watercolour design for a block-printed fabric manufactured by G. P. & J. Baker in 1903. It is likely that the use of colour washes in textile designs of this period was inspired by architectural drawings. This encouraged the use of new techniques, such as rainbow printing, to achieve such effects.

10. Lindsay P. Butterfield: roller-printed cotton manufactured by Turnbull and Stockdale, 1901. The pattern was also used for wallpaper.

11. Lindsay P. Butterfield: block-printed linen manufactured by G. P. & J. Baker, 1903. The pattern was printed with a solid ground from 1904.

12. C. F. A. Voysey: 'Daisy', silk and wool double cloth woven by Alexander Morton & Co., c. 1898.

13. C. F. A. Voysey: sample strip of colourways for a silk and wool double cloth from Alexander Morton & Co.'s 'Helena' range, c. 1895-1900.

14. Lewis F. Day: roller-printed cotton manufactured by Turnbull and Stockdale in 1888, probably shown at the first Arts and Crafts Exhibition.

15. Arthur Silver: 'Peacock Feather', roller-printed cotton manufactured for Liberty's by the Rossendale Printing Co. c. 1887, and shown that year at the Manchester Royal Jubilee Exhibition.

16. George C. Haité: 'Crocus', block-printed by G. P. & J. Baker in 1903 on a cotton and linen fabric with a woven figured ground. The effects of shaded colour or rainbow printing can be seen in a number of fabrics at this time.

17. Lewis F. Day: 'Tulip Tree', roller-printed cotton manufactured by Turnbull and Stockdale in 1903.

9

10

11

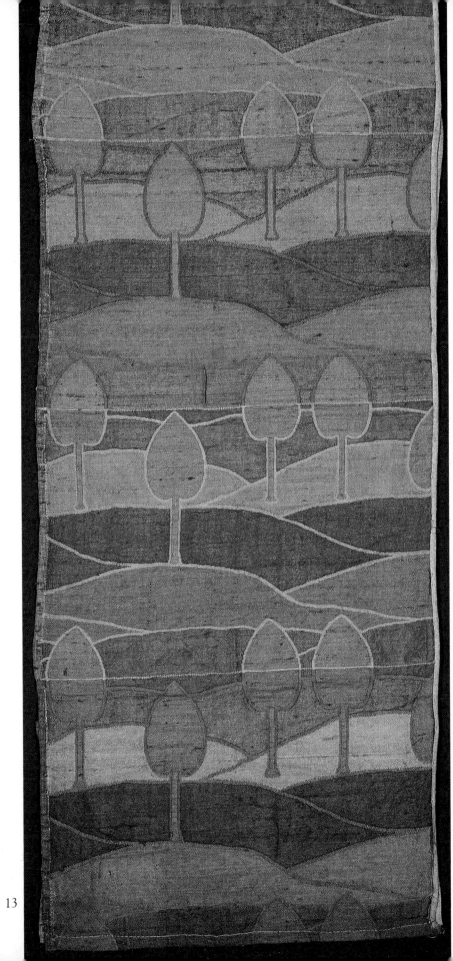

16

17

1 The Artistic and Industrial Background

HE years between the Great Exhibition of 1851 and the first Arts and Crafts Exhibition in 1888 saw changes in the style and structure of British textiles made both in the factory and at home. The controlling factor was generally fashion, but other forms of interference from outside the industry also had a considerable bearing on its overall development.

Henry Cole's energetic attempts to improve the design of industrial art in the 1840s and 1850s had little direct effect on textile production. The firm he established, Summerly's Art Manufactures, is not known to have produced textile designs, and while he selected some printed cottons for his 1852 exhibition *False Principles of Design* to show their 'Direct Imitation of Nature', this only reinforced existing criticism that three-dimensionally realistic floral motifs were unsuitable for mass-produced furnishings.[1] It was left, therefore, to the published works of such influential theorists as Owen Jones to explain how improved designs should be applied, although he was not specific in identifying the technical processes for which his ideas were intended.

From an early age designers were not encouraged to experiment with pattern and technique. This showed particularly in the work of students from the various national Schools of Design in which Henry Cole had a controlling interest for several years. Developed around industrial centres, these schools concentrated on the production of patterns which suited local industry (to try to ensure future employment). They also taught students all the processes involved in transforming their designs into finished goods. What they did not do was encourage originality in design or the use of new techniques which could develop those industries further. Such complacency meant that the appearance of textiles varied very little in the period 1851-70 and despite criticism from artistic quarters the prevailing concern of manufacturers was the search for cheaper methods, more unnatural technical effects and brighter colours.

Some limited improvement in textile design had been seen from the middle of the century with the introduction of geometric patterns inspired by the work of the architects A. W. N. Pugin and Owen Jones, and for a time the two popular elements of floral and geometric ornament were produced side-by-side. It is difficult to assess how much direct influence Pugin had in this field. Whereas his ecclesiastical designs were of paramount importance in the revival of church ornament (and many of his published motifs were copied directly for church embroidery), as an architect his interest in textiles never extended beyond their use as one element in his decorative schemes. It is this factor above all others that separates his work from that of the group of architects designing textiles at the end of the nineteenth century. Pugin had no first-hand practical experience of techniques. He was however always quite specific about the type of cloth he required his two furnishers, Crace and Hardman, to manufacture from his patterns, although he did select textures and finishes already in production.

Owen Jones's greatest influence was through his books of ornamental details, particularly those taken from the Alhambra (1842),[2] and those assembled in his wider-ranging *Grammar of Ornament* (1856), which was illustrated in chromolithography. The latter was to be found in the libraries of most free-lance designers and the studios of large factories throughout the late nineteenth and early twentieth centuries. Although it is known that Jones himself supplied designs to several firms producing printed and woven textiles and carpets, patterns from his books were widely copied so identification of his own original work is almost impossible. Patterns drawn by him can be identified from the existing records of only two silk manufacturers, Daniel Walters & Sons of Braintree and Warner & Ramm,[3] so it is difficult to discover whether his interest in the production of textiles was carried beyond their surface pattern.

Christopher Dresser, writing some years later in such publications as *Principles of Decorative Design* (1873),[4] did apply his ideas to particular objects, carpets for instance, but his designs did not take into consideration the tactile qualities of the textiles: they simply showed the effect of using flat patterns on familiar furnishings made in techniques already in use at that time.

Silk was very fashionable for costumes and furnishings, and its use by designers such as Pugin to decorate artistic homes only added to its popularity. The British silk industry, however, was not the main beneficiary. Already weakened by the appeal of the prohibition on French imports, which took effect in 1826, it received a further blow in 1860 with the signing of Cobden's treaty in which the 15% duty levied on the import of foreign silks was abolished. In the first year imports almost doubled.[5] British manufacturers badly needed protection from their French competitors, as manufacturers in Lyons could produce hand-woven silks more cheaply than in Britain, and Paris dictated fashion. The industries of Spitalfields, Coventry, Dublin, Derby and Macclesfield all suffered greatly, some irretrievably, by the slump which followed. Soon many British firms, unable to stand the competition, went out of business, despite a short respite in 1870 caused by the Franco-Prussian war. The few British companies still in production by the 1870s were ones which concentrated on specific corners of the market, with those in Macclesfield producing cheap men's dress accessories, for instance, and in Coventry specializing in the picture ribbon trade. A small group of silk manufacturers continued to weave for the top end of the interior design market, and of these Daniel Walters & Sons were particularly sensible in restricting their production to luxury goods. Surprisingly, the temporary contraction of French imports in 1870 encouraged one particular Spitalfields weaver, Benjamin Warner, to start production and within a few years Warner, Sillett & Ramm became one of the most successful suppliers to the fashionable retail trade. Like Walters, Warner offered a large range of both traditional and modern designs and thus could compete on equal terms with foreign manufacturers.

Because of the dictates of fashion, the Lancashire cotton industry did not immediately benefit from the contraction of the British silk industry. Whereas the 1840s and 1850s had proved the high point for British floral chintz (glazed cotton), printed fabrics were little used for costumes of the 1860s and 1870s and had only limited summer use in the home. In the 1860s the standard of design and printing was low and Lancashire depended on the sale of vast quantities of cottons made especially for export to keep the industry afloat. This it managed despite increasing competition from Alsatian and other French printers in both the home and export markets. Its survival was fortunate, for in the mid-1870s there was a revival in the use of printed cottons for furnishings (now called 'cretonnes') which lasted well into the twentieth century.

Not all sections of the textile industry were affected in these ways. Carpet manufacture flourished in a climate which appreciated eclecticism. Most firms were able to provide a wide range of machine-made types (Brussels, Axminsters, Wiltons and Kidderminsters) which satisfied all levels of the market. Some manufacturers capitalized on this success and one Glasgow firm, Templeton's, attempted to expand the range of its goods further with a successful though short-lived venture into the production of woven *portières*. Other long-established firms, including the printers Thomas Clarkson of Bannister Hall, Stead McAlpin of Carlisle and the Yorkshire woollen mills of H. C. McCrea and J. W. & C. Ward, managed without such gimmicks and, despite strong buffeting by fashion and outside competition, continued to produce the high quality goods for which they had originally earned their reputations.

The popularity of Japanese-inspired patterns from the late 1860s provided a means of limited recovery for sections of the printing and weaving industries. The earliest and best designs in this style were British, by the architects E. W. Godwin and B. J. Talbert and the botanist Christopher Dresser. All three worked for both woven and printed textile manufacturers and Dresser provided patterns for various techniques including carpets, woven bedspreads and damask table linen.

A growing interest in the decorative motifs of the Near and Far East led to the establishment of shops specializing in the import and sale of Eastern goods. Liberty's in Regent Street, opened in 1875, is the best known name today, but at the time it was only one of a number of retail establishments dealing in such 'curios'.

The versatility of the leading exponents of the Aesthetic Movement, who applied their talents to all branches of decoration, had a marked effect on the practice of future designers: textiles were seen as important objects in their own right and not mere backdrops. The industry also benefited from the enlightened attitude of many manufacturers who recognized the advantages of buying good free-lance designs. However, despite the improvement in patterns and colours (and palettes were considerably restricted from this time), fashionable textiles remained very similar in structure to those of the middle of the century. Only the dramatic changes brought about by a totally new attitude to manufacture and interior design enabled British textiles to satisfy an increasingly restless market at home and abroad.

In 1875 William Morris established his second firm, Morris & Co. Through early experiments in making and decorating cloth (embroideries in particular) he had developed a positive idea of the types of textiles he wished to use in his own home, and eventually to offer for sale. Reacting against commercially available furnishings, he realized that any improvement in colour, pattern and texture would involve studying the basic elements of technique used in production. His interest in and knowledge of historic design had led him,

18. Alexander Morton, posing in front of a Donegal carpet loom at Killybegs.

in the last years of the 1860s, to commission the manufacturer Thomas Clarkson to reproduce three of that firm's block-printed cottons of the 1830s for him to sell in his Queen Square shop, and it was such early techniques as block-printing that Morris subsequently adopted for his own textiles. He found that these not only provided more pleasing effects but also allowed the craftsman (whether designer, printer, weaver or embroiderer) better control over the translation of designs and the entire manufacturing process. He preferred the effects of block-printing to the engraved roller, which had been widely adopted for cheapness and efficiency. Morris's abhorrence of bright artificial dyestuffs led him to investigate natural dyes (indigo, madder and weld in particular), which had all been used at the beginning of the century but were now almost obsolete. His initial experiments with Thomas Wardle, at Wardle's dye works at Leek in Staffordshire, are well chronicled through correspondence and dye books which reveal the energy and enthusiasm of the two men in their search for the colourings and effects they desired. Despite displays of artistic temperament from time to time this cooperation, which involved both men toiling day after day with recipes and dye vats, can be seen as the first practical manifestation of the principles of the Arts and Crafts Movement, some thirteen years before the Society was formed.

Morris was excited by the texture and tactile qualities of cloth and designed a great number of different types of woven textiles using natural fibres. These were wool double and triple cloths, silk and cotton lenos (gauzes), silk and wool double cloths, silk, cotton, wool and mohair damasks, brocaded velvets, silk and linen mixtures and silk and wool compound weaves. With the exception of triple cloths, silk and wool double cloths and lenos, all the fabrics were made, at one time or another, at the firm's factory at Merton Abbey in Wimbledon near London which Morris leased from 1881. This list represents a vast range for one shop, let alone a single manufacturer, and was only partially approached in the variety of techniques used by French weavers in the Lille area. If one adds to it the firm's production of embroideries, tapestries, printed cottons, linens, wools and challis (silk and wool) and hand-knotted and machine-woven carpeting it is possible to get some idea of the originality and versatility of Morris as a textile manufacturer.

Morris reviled the working conditions in northern mills brought about chiefly by the use of steam power. Yet although he used hand-operated jacquards at Merton Abbey he was not in principle opposed to power looms, feeling that if properly controlled they would be more efficient and equally effective. Some of the fabrics made by outside contractors for the firm were produced by this method.

It must not be forgotten that although Morris's influence over contemporary designers and manufacturers was great, during his own lifetime his work affected only a small section of the market – part of the fashionable artistic interior design trade. However, it was through his followers, textile manufacturers throughout Great Britain and fellow members of the Arts and Crafts Exhibition Society, that the true importance of his contribution to the arts of the day was finally recognized.

The organization of the Merton Abbey Works, which provided attractive surroundings and interesting work as an incentive to achieve uncompromisingly good results, was imitated by various other firms, and also by newly-established companies. Thomas Wardle developed a natural dyeing section alongside more commercial production and, as well as continuing to print the popular Eastern patterns associated with his name, he increased his purchasing of original patterns by leading designers. The modernization of the Turnbull and Stockdale print works in Stacksteads, Lancashire, saw that firm become a major supplier of cretonnes, especially of the new reversible fabrics, under the guidance of Lewis F. Day, who was appointed Artistic Director in 1881. Significantly, a number of small specialist weaving firms were opened at this time, notably Arthur H. Lee & Sons, first in Lancashire and later in Cheshire. Alexander Morton, whose factory had developed from the local muslin industry of his home town of Darvel in Ayrshire, in time became one of the largest and most successful manufacturers of woven textiles and carpets (and later printed textiles). Like Lee, Morton founded his works with Morris's principles in mind. All the firms mentioned became frequent participants in the various Arts and Crafts Exhibitions, and it is the working practices which they adopted and the designs which they used that influenced British industry well into the twentieth century.

Hand embroidery in the nineteenth century showed little originality and a gradual degeneration of skills before the artistic re-appraisal of the craft in the 1870s. Although embroidery became more widely practised than ever before, one single technique, tent and cross stitch in wool on canvas, swamped the haberdashers' shelves and occupied all the waking hours of the embroideress. (The expansion in the nineteenth century of the craft's amateur status meant that such work was associated, quite correctly, with women.) From the early years of the century canvases and wool were imported from Germany, and the method continued to be called 'Berlin woolwork' despite the involvement of British manufacturers from the 1830s. Little skill was required to copy the patterns, but the technique took such a hold on one of the most traditional of all British crafts that, as late as 1885, *Kelly's Directory* listed commercial embroidery stores under the title 'Berlin Warehouses'.

A reaction by Morris and some of his contemporaries led to embroidery of a different kind being created, first in the home (by the wives, daughters and sisters of artists and designers) and later professionally. Commercially referred to as 'Art Needlework', this included all surface techniques but instead of counting threads embroideresses translated their designs (provided by the leading artistic figures of the day) in a much freer way than before, choosing outline or filling stitches according to the effects they wanted. Colouring was also an important factor and in an effort to get away from the brash unnatural anilines of the wools in canvas work kits, pale shades of gold, sepia, ochre and olive green (first made popular by artists of the Aesthetic Movement) were used in the 1870s, giving way in the 1880s to the natural hues advocated by Morris.

A number of ladies' embroidery societies were started in the 1870s, the earliest being the Royal School of Art Needlework, founded in 1872. Run on charitable lines, these professional organizations soon took commercial advantage of the new style. The Royal School, the Ladies' Work Society and the Decorative Needlework Society were all frequent exhibitors with the Arts and Crafts Society, and they, together with the many talented amateurs of the period, helped to re-establish embroidery as a technique worthy of the highest regard.

2 The Evolution of a Style

HAVING suggested in the Preface that the Arts and Crafts Movement has no one discernible style or image, it is important to explain, before examining the textiles of the Arts and Crafts Exhibitions more fully, the main characteristics which epitomize the work of the designers and craftsmen involved. Enough similarities do occur for many of the products to be recognized as contemporary with one another, and the patterns used show sympathetic approaches both in the choice of subject-matter and in technique.

The nineteenth century is always looked upon as a period of intense eclecticism, and it is true that the majority of textiles of the first eighty years show designs based on historic styles or foreign patterns or a mixture of these. Such fashions came in waves, and often recurred. In the first half of the century people preferred their patterns to have a European source (anything from the medieval to the late eighteenth-century), with only rare excursions to Egypt, China or Turkey. Later, manufacturers concentrated on patterns from the Far East – first China, then Japan – and then from the countries of the Near and Middle East. This widening of artistic boundaries had much to do with the opening and expansion of travel around the world and Britain's increasing foreign trade.

The import of numerous goods from overseas meant that the general public soon became familiar with Oriental styles, and manufacturers and retailers found that such patterns were extremely popular, whether offered for sale in their original 'undiluted' form or adapted for the home market. Thomas Wardle was particularly interested in Indian textiles and travelled throughout India and the Near and Middle East collecting patterns and strengthening trade links with foreign manufacturers. He imported quantities of Indian silks (both plain and with woven designs) and dyed and printed these at his dye works at Leek.[1] They found a ready market through Liberty's shop in Regent Street which, in the 1870s and 1880s, specialized in Eastern goods, and one of his imported silks, 'Tanjore Lotus', provided the shop with its early trade-mark.[2] Another firm with strong Eastern connections was G. P. & J. Baker, founded by two brothers born and brought up in Turkey, who began trading in London as 'warehousemen' and importers of goods from that country. Their first designs as manufacturers were based on Turkish patterns and they continued to retain similar ones in their range for many years.

Although William Morris's historic preferences lay in the arts of medieval England and France, his textiles were strongly influenced by fifteenth-, sixteenth- and seventeenth-century Italian woven fabrics and, towards the end of his career, by the patterns of Persia and Turkey. That he was also interested in the Indian textiles he saw whilst working with

19. 'Tanjore Lotus', tusser silk with a woven design, c. 1880, imported from India by Thomas Wardle and sold through Liberty's.

20. William Morris: 'Indian Diaper', block-printed cotton manufactured by Morris & Co., designed late in 1875 when Morris was working at Leek with Wardle.

21. Thomas Wardle: block-printed Indian tusser silk showing the influence of Persian decoration, c.1878. A variation of this design was shown at the 1888 and 1890 Exhibitions.

Thomas Wardle in Leek in 1875 appears especially in the scale and colouring of a small group of his patterns from that period. Morris and Wardle were, therefore, continuing a long tradition in using existing patterns as the source of inspiration, but they were more selective and original in their approach. Exotic designs remained in fashion to the end of the nineteenth century and although not a direct element in Arts and Crafts textiles, their influence as precursors is important. The lessons learned from studying these helped to promote new techniques, and with the gradual understanding of tried and tested pattern repeats the designer developed a confidence not experienced for many generations. With confidence came new ideas and with the acceptance and encouragement of more innovative patterns by both industry and the buying public a totally original image was born.

20

22. C. F. A. Voysey, drawn by Harold
Speed in 1896.

Fine draughtsmanship is one of the most important characteristics of Arts and Crafts patterns and it is interesting to note just how many of the designers involved received a traditional artistic training, whether as an architect or through the various Schools of Design. The basic elements which combine to make the pure naturalistic style of the Movement can be seen as early as 1856 in Christopher Dresser's detailed drawings of the horsechestnut tree combined in a full-page illustration in Owen Jones's *Grammar of Ornament*.[3] Although Jones used these drawings to show that geometry is the basis of all symmetrical and regular design, the unmistakable love of nature and Dresser's botanical knowledge of the tree's growth are at the heart of their success as works of art and inspirations for pattern. Earlier Victorian artists were certainly capable of representing natural form: in fact their renditions are usually too good when used as repeating designs because the floral details completely dominate any overall scheme. Printed, woven and embroidered in a number of different effects with raised techniques and bright aniline dyes, they are uncomfortably three-dimensional and life-like. It is this quality in pattern-making above all else that Henry Cole and Christopher Dresser criticized and that was eventually eradicated in art education.

The naturalistic style perfected for textiles of the Arts and Crafts Movement is epitomized in the work of three people, Lindsay P. Butterfield, George C. Haité and C. F. A. 23,130 Voysey (a designer, a painter and an architect). With an economy of line and a deliberate 22

11,12, avoidance of three-dimensional effects they achieved a far more natural, original and
16 pleasing result. This approach was not arrived at in a gimmicky way but grew from a
thorough knowledge of both subject-matter and technique.

Changing fashions in garden design and an interest in plants contributed to this style
and show in the choice of subjects and in the manner in which these are portrayed.
Mid-Victorian textiles were overwhelmed by exotic brightly coloured plants, particularly
those grown in unnatural conditions in hot-houses. Endless sources for design were provided by the Royal Botanic Gardens who sponsored collecting expeditions abroad between
1842 and 1863. Favourite subjects included pelargoniums, fuchsias, rhododendrons, hyd-
rangeas, lilies, orchids and an abundance of the new tea-roses, grouped closely together or
in trailing designs combined with *trompe-l'oeil* representations of ribbons and lace. An
interest in Japanese design led to simplification in line and colour in the 1870s. Only plants
from the East or those which would adapt to this comparatively stark style were chosen,
especially forsythia, magnolia, chrysanthemums, jasmine and willow branches.

The naturally trailing stems of jasmine provided William Morris with his first repeating
pattern for a fabric but it was his choice of British flowers, many from the hedgerows of the
countryside, which had the most abiding influence on British textile design from the 1870s
until the second decade of the twentieth century. This British phenomenon arose from new
attitudes to horticulture and from the increasing importance of the flower-filled garden as
part of the architectural setting of the fashionable home. Gardens became more random
in appearance though painstaking in planning. William Robinson in his books, *Alpine
Flowers for English Gardens* (1870) and *The English Flower Garden* (1883), advocated a
wilder and more natural effect than had been seen before. Averse to the seasonal bedding
out of plants started in the greenhouse, Robinson felt that the garden should reflect the
normal effects of the weather and helped to set a fashion for sweeping lawns, beds of shrubs
and hardy plants and walls covered with flowering creepers.

Morris's own love of gardening is evident in all his repeating designs and his use of less
familiar flowers provided an endless variety of forms. The plants he preferred were those
established in Great Britain for many centuries, though some had fallen from popularity
since the seventeenth century. He utilized the familiar shapes of marigolds, tulips, car-
nations and anemones but gained a more individual effect by combining these with
columbines, snakeshead fritillaries, larkspur, borage and crown imperials, all rather
more reminiscent of Elizabethan embroidery than anything available in England in his
own time. He was particularly fond of the curving leaves of the acanthus and the trailing
branches of willow and honeysuckle which he used time and time again both as the
main theme of designs and in subsidiary backgrounds.

It is not surprising, therefore, to find that many of the later designers of repeating floral
23 patterns were also keen gardeners and chose the subjects of their designs on a basis of
8,9 botanical and horticultural knowledge. The patterns of Butterfield and Haité in particular
show clear crisp linear drawings of flowers and other natural details in washes of flat, even
colour, their attractiveness lying in their representation of the subject, capturing its natural
growth and essential characteristics. There is very little attempt to distort or adapt for the
24,25 sake of pattern and all the flowers, plants, trees and fruit used are shown at their best, in bud
or full bloom, reflected in the light of an English spring or summer morning. Plants selected

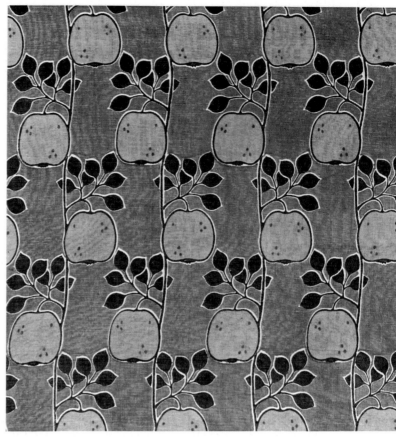

23. Lindsay P. Butterfield in his garden.

24. Lindsay P. Butterfield: 'Apple', block-printed linen manufactured by G. P. & J. Baker c. 1898 and sold through Heal's until 1908. A woven version was manufactured by Alexander Morton & Co. in their 'Ivegill' range.

25. Silk, wool and cotton double cloth, probably designed by Lindsay P. Butterfield, woven by Alexander Morton & Co., c. 1900.

continued the fashion for traditional garden flowers and fritillaries, pansies, forget-me-nots, crocus, daffodils and tulips were used with less familiar images like honesty, teazle, 125 hemlock and briony. Tall and trailing plants provided invaluable frameworks and, whereas Morris had mostly used curving leaves to control his patterns, stems now formed repeats and provided movement. It is these elements above all others which give the style an 26-29 intensely British quality and one that excited foreign buyers by its originality.

Manufacturers showed a similar interest in translating these designs with highly successful results. G. P. Baker, the son of a professional gardener, retained a passion for plants throughout his long life. He was a keen and notable collector of alpine plants and a hybridizer of iris, and one can easily detect among the designs produced by his firm those which were chosen by him.[4] Alexander Morton spent many years perfecting commercial dyestuffs and his results go further than those of any other weaver in reproducing the subtle, mellow yet rich hues of the designs.

The influence of William Robinson's views on gardening was unabated until the 1890s when two new publications, *Garden Craft Old and New* by J. D. Sedding (1891) and Reginald Blomfield's *The Formal Garden in England* (1892), developed Robinson's work in a more formal setting. A number of architects favoured this approach for it was more in keeping with building designs of the period. Those like Voysey who also designed repeating patterns adopted many of these later ideas, for instance topiary.

26. (*opposite*) John Illingworth Kay: 'Lily', block-printed silk bedcover manufactured at the Swaisland Print Works of G. P. & J. Baker in 1893. Covers of this type were sold through Liberty's, Heal's and Story's shops (see, e.g., Ill. 123).

27. Allan Vigers: 'Mallory', or 'Rose and Pansy', watercolour design, 1901, sold to G. P. & J. Baker and produced as a block-printed linen. Shown at the 1903 Exhibition as 'Rose'.

28. Lewis F. Day: 'Daffodils', block-printed velveteen manufactured by Turnbull and Stockdale, c. 1888.

29. Roller-printed cotton, a 'Liberty Art Fabric', originally sold at 1*s*. 4*d*. a yard. Bought from the shop in 1894 by Manchester School of Art.

Whereas the type of floral decoration created by Butterfield, Haité and Voysey characterized the middle period of the Arts and Crafts Movement (approximately from 1893 to 1903) and is its most typical and original form, earlier and later textiles were much more dependent on existing styles. The naturalism of Morris and the eccentric but original ideas of the short-lived Century Guild combined to influence such designers as Lewis F. Day and Sidney Mawson who, although active in the early 1880s, were still designing well into the twentieth century. Both produced patterns based on the Morris format of natural motifs within a formal framework. Many of their designs were printed (by Wardle and by Turnbull and Stockdale) in the revived technique of indigo discharge favoured by Morris. Mawson's 62 patterns in the 1880s were so closely based on Morris's that they can be (and on occasions 30 have been) mistaken for his work. His designs lacked Morris's draughtsmanship, however, and it is his later, more original, work that contributed constructively to the Arts and 138 Crafts Movement. Day, who was also an eclectic designer, provided a set of very original and attractive designs for Turnbull and Stockdale between 1882 and c. 1907. In these he used the sinuous curving forms first seen in the work of A. H. Mackmurdo of the Century 60,61, Guild, who is now recognized to have been an important contributing influence on later 63 Continental Art Nouveau designs. Day's patterns have swirling acanthus leaves with 14,105 superimposed lace-like veining in both formal turn-over and freer meandering repeats.

In the first few years of the twentieth century Arts and Crafts designs in turn responded to the 'New Art' from the Continent. A few British designers, such as Harry Napper (who had recently left the Silver Studio to work on a free-lance basis), drew some amazing patterns in which floral motifs took on unnatural geometric and angular forms. Many of his 31

30. Sidney Mawson: 'Tiger Lily', indigo discharge (see Ill. 62) and block-printed cotton manufactured by Thomas Wardle, c. 1890.

31. Silver Studio (probably Harry Napper): 'Santiago', cotton fabric woven in northern France, c. 1905.

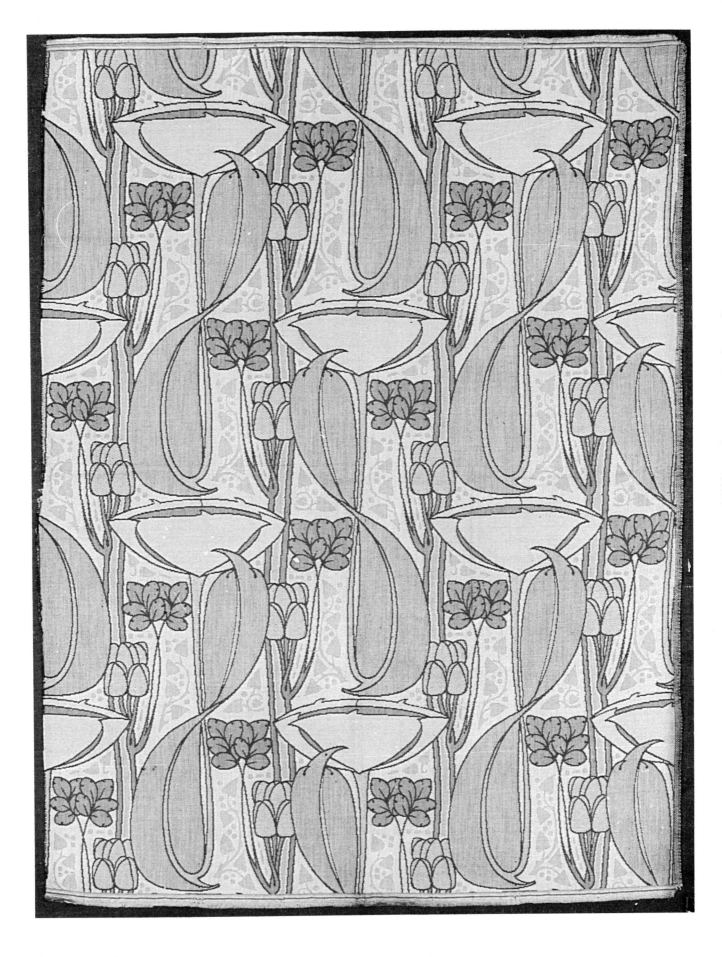

32. Ann Macbeth: 'St Elizabeth', c.1900, worked on satin in silks, gold thread, seed pearls, gold beads and translucent stones by Elizabeth Jackson.

33. Ann Macbeth, wearing an embroidered collar of her own design, c.1908.

patterns were sold to the French.[5] Some British manufacturers, including F. Steiner of 108-11 Church, near Accrington in Lancashire, printed large ranges of cottons from such designs especially for the Continental market.[6]

Of greater influence outside Britain at the end of the nineteenth century was decorative work devised by artists and designers associated with the Glasgow School of Art. This was also based upon naturalistic motifs, particularly rosebuds, but often so stylized that they border on abstraction. The four main exponents of the style, Charles Rennie Mackintosh, Herbert McNair and Frances and Margaret Macdonald, designed few repeating patterns in the important early years:[7] their textile work then consisted chiefly of isolated examples of 42,69 stencilled linen and embroidery. The style was more fully realized in the embroideries of 32,33, Jessie Newbery, Ann Macbeth and their students at the Glasgow School of Art. The 82-5 Scottish manufacturer Alexander Morton also adopted a number of similar patterns, many drawn by his nephew, Gavin Morton, and used them for woven textiles and hand-knotted and machine-woven carpets.

34. Century Guild (Herbert Horne):
'The Angel with the Trumpet', block-
printed cotton manufactured by
Simpson & Godlee from 1884, probably
shown by the Guild at the 1888
Exhibition.

Unfortunately, Glasgow work had little effect on English designs, and with the diminution of a strongly characteristic style English patterns continued to follow current gardening fashions. Gertrude Jekyll, who had studied under Robinson, combined elements of both his and later theories in her own gardening and was also a talented embroideress. Textiles from the period 1905-1915 reflect this mixture of styles with a return to more conventional patterns. The later fashion for Italianate schemes led to the introduction of representations of sculpture and garden furniture.

In addition to ideas derived from gardens, Arts and Crafts textiles made use of figures, 34 animals and birds. Herbert Horne had drawn a repeating design, 'The Angel with the Trumpet', as early as 1884 and figures were included most successfully in tapestries and embroideries. The main impetus for using these motifs in repeating designs came from those involved in book illustration. The rise in popularity of pictorial children's books 35 provided one of the Movement's most influential designers, Walter Crane, who took many of the subjects of his patterns directly from his own illustrations. His style is particularly

35. Walter Crane: 'The Colonies', roller-printed cotton manufactured by Edmund Potter & Co. Designed for the Royal Jubilee of 1887 and registered on 20 May. The pattern was described at the time as 'a kind of apotheosis of the British Empire expressed in a figurative way.'

68 well suited to embroidery and linen damasks where his complicated compositions can best
be seen. Léon Victor Solon (who had worked for a number of years as a designer of
36 ceramics) in his only known textile design beats Crane at his own game, combining an
enviable ability to draw figures with strong decorative quality; Wardle increased its attrac-
tion yet further by adding a small floral border[8] when it was printed as a scarf.

73-76   Embroideries depicting figures take on many forms. Early copies of paintings done by
the Royal School of Art Needlework were executed mostly in long and short stitches in
wools and silks covering the entire surface of the ground. Later figurative panels show more
32 intuitive techniques such as appliqué, used so successfully by Godfrey Blount for his robust
59 peasants seen for instance in 'The Spies'.

36. Léon Victor Solon:
block-printed silk square
manufactured by Thomas
Wardle, with a border
designed by him.
Registered in December
1893 and shown as a
velveteen at that year's
Exhibition.

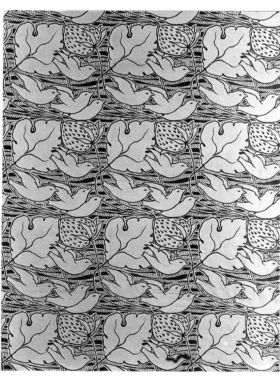

now sit and see · nor ride nor haste

37. 'The Forest' silk and wool tapestry, designed by William Morris and J. H. Dearle with animals by Philip Webb, 1887. Shown by Morris & Co. at the 1888 and 1889 Exhibitions.

38. C. F. A. Voysey: 'The Owl', woollen fabric woven by Alexander Morton & Co. in 1898 as part of their 'Abbotsford' range. The design was also sold to Essex & Co. for use as a wallpaper.

39. C. F. A. Voysey: roller-printed cotton manufactured by Newman, Smith and Newman in 1897.

40. 'See-Saw', design for a roller-printed nursery cushion cover manufactured by G. P. & J. Baker in 1903 for Liberty's. Possibly drawn by William Kidd.

One of the finest individual designs incorporating animals and birds is 'The Forest' 37 tapestry, woven in 1887 by Morris & Co. Voysey is the bird and animal designer *par excellence* and his ability to control patterns including figures, animals, birds and flowers has 38,39 never been matched. His highly original inventions have humour and a strong narrative 53-5, quality and despite their almost nursery-like character they are sophisticated and never 151 mawkish.

The new interest in decoration for children, with special wallpaper friezes and novel ideas for the nursery, led to the working of a number of embroideries for this purpose, many of which were shown at the Arts and Crafts Exhibitions. A series of cushion covers printed by G. P. & J. Baker at their Swaisland Print Works show nursery-rhymes and scenes with Dutch children probably drawn by the popular illustrators Cecil Aldrin and William Kidd. 40 These proved very successful in the first few years of the twentieth century and were advertised in a number of Liberty's catalogues.

Having discussed the subjects chosen for the textile designs of the Arts and Crafts Movement, a little more should be said about the types of fabrics which were selected and how these were used in the home.

During the 1880s lighter interiors began to supplant the rich, cluttered, rather sombre effects favoured by the mid-Victorians. Morris had done much to revive the use of printed fabrics for furnishings, and schemes carried out by Morris & Co. (particularly in houses designed by Philip Webb) show an abundance of white paintwork with colour provided by carefully selected carpets and other textiles. Heavier materials remained fashionable, with corduroys, velveteen and woven fabrics being used for curtains, *portières* and upholstery. Printed velveteen was very popular and 'reckoned to be among the arts of the country',[9] but despite good designs from Morris & Co., Thomas Wardle, and Turnbull and Stockdale, the majority of English-designed velveteens sold in London shops were made in France.

As late as 1888 fashionable interior design was still dictated by traditional furnishers and articles in ladies' magazines. Advice given in such influential periodicals as *The Queen* not only stipulated colours for each season but, in response to the briefest of descriptions, told correspondents what fabrics should be used in their home. In the issue for 13 October, that closest to the first Arts and Crafts Exhibition, the colours set for the coming winter included 'Chartreuse, crevette, maize, nil, cythère – a new green, Saxe – a deep blue, suède, mouthe – a greyish blue and écorne', denoting a strong French influence. The correspondence columns gave wide-ranging advice on textiles and were even-handed with their recommendations of the leading shops. Their suggestions included the use of Liberty's Medicis velvets (to hide shabby ends of curtains), Shoolbred's Medicis or Florentine damask brocades and 'dainty small chrysanthemum cretonnes', yellow and white 'art' muslin, creamy Madras muslin, Graham and Biddle's poinsettia cretonne, 'Debenham and Freebody's . . . handsome printed velveteens suitable for drapery', and Holroyd Barker's mosque chenille curtains to use as throw-over coverings for sofas.

The partial revival of silk weaving in Britain was dominated in the early years by the production of fashionable light-weight 'art' silks which, surprisingly, had a number of uses in the home. A printed velveteen produced by Wardle for the Aesthetic Gallery, now in the Victoria and Albert Museum, is trimmed with a deep golden yellow border. Fine silk 57,123 bedcovers and hangings were printed by G. P. & J. Baker for both Heal's and Liberty's.[10] Whereas one cannot compare the industry of 1891, when approximately 80 looms were in production, to that thirty years earlier when 160 mills and factories employed over 56,000 people,[11] the efforts of Wardle and fellow members of the Silk Association had a considerable success and English silk began to regain its place as the most popular luxury furnishing.

An increasing interest in weaving at this time is also illustrated by reports in the press concerning ingenious inventions for the loom. Jan Szczepanik's new photographic method used in the preparation of patterns enabled a design 35 inches (89 cm) square to be adapted in six hours instead of weeks,[12] and improvements to the jacquard loom patented by Flather & Sons of Bradford allowed a greater speed of production with less friction on the fibres.[13]

In the latter part of the nineteenth century architects and fashionable London shops dictated interior decoration. Much of their advice expressed a new feeling for healthy and hygienic living and their aim was to produce a light and airy atmosphere. This attitude, fostered by a refound interest in the countryside, had a marked effect on the designs of furnishing textiles and the choice of fabrics used. Advice about the appearance of houses was quite specific. G. F. Armitage, an art teacher and supplier of designs to industry, set out his views in a lecture delivered in Manchester in 1885.[14] He told the public 'to select the most cheerful, light-giving colours and combine them in perfect harmonies. Be sure that few things are more injurious to health . . . than dark heavy inharmonious colours, and the combinations of strong opposites.' Aymer Vallance, writing in the *Art Journal* in 1892,[15] expanded this theme: 'In the country there is nothing more fresh and homely than the old fashioned white dimity, but for smoky towns something with a pattern, like a cretonne is more serviceable, because it does not show the dirt so quickly.' He believed that curtains should be short (just long enough to touch the sill), and if used on doors should not graze the floor, for large, heavy drapes excluded fresh air and harboured dust. Shorter curtains hung better (only a little fullness was suggested) and did not need the trimmings or ties so popular in the earlier part of the century. He believed that tassels, braids, cord and chains 'only added to the expense, the snobbishness and the unhealthiness of a room without in any way adding to its beauty'. Printed cottons and gauzes became the most popular choice for curtains, and woven fabrics, thought to create a 'close and dusty atmosphere', were used chiefly for upholstery. With the increase in hand jacquard weaving a certain prestige was attached to those products, which were referred to as 'hand-woven'.[16] Liberty's 41 nevertheless used hand-woven as well as power-loom-woven fabrics on chairs with very successful results.

Most of the houses built at this time had wholesome and practical features such as 44 casement windows and upholstered window seats, many of which needed fabric for decoration and comfort. The mixture of old and new ideas incorporated in many of these 'country cottages' conformed to what Walter Crane called 'the older and simpler English Manner'.[17] The re-awakened passion for simplicity and purity of detail was not appreciated by

41. Liberty armchairs, c.1906, upholstered with power- and hand-jacquard-woven woollen fabrics by Alexander Morton & Co. from designs by Allan Vigers, C. F. A. Voysey, Joseph Doran and Gavin Morton.

42. Herbert McNair and Frances Macdonald: wooden settle with leaded glass decoration and appliqué upholstery, c.1900.

43. Oak bedsteads with covers and hangings of Haslemere 'Peasant Tapestries', shown by Heal's at the Paris Exhibition in 1900.

everyone. The *Magazine of Art*, reporting on the 1896 Arts and Crafts Exhibition, wrote that it had led some members of the Society 'into a selfconscious baldness that resulted in what is dubbed the "rabbit-hutch" school'.[18]

Printed cottons with white and pale grounds were increasingly used throughout the house, and more attention was given to bedrooms. Heal's, famed for its hygienic mattresses, sold a range of suitable bedroom furnishings including printed cotton and silk bedcovers. They also sold appliqué hangings from Haslemere which were acceptable 43 hygienically because they were made from washable linen. Unfitted carpet squares, permitting the easy cleaning of the wooden floors around, became fashionable, and some washable fabrics were even suggested for wall decoration.

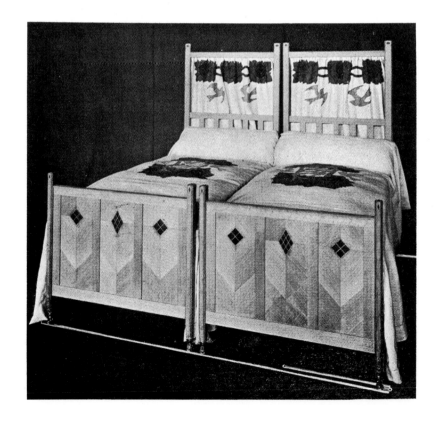

A Casement Window.

The short curtain blinds are here made of HEAL & SON'S CASEMENT FLAX dyed a plain shade or in the "natural" colour. The long curtains are of the same material printed with a simple design.

A Sash Window.

This shows the adaptation to sash windows; the upper curtains are drawn by a light pulley and line.

For prices of Rods and Fixings see page 101.

44. Advertisement for curtains from Heal's *A Book of Bedroom Furniture*, 1903.

45. Settle designed by A. H. Mackmurdo for Morris & Co. with upholstery and furnishings of Morris's 'Tulip' printed cotton. It was bought from the firm's Oxford Street shop c. 1893.

46. Window in the master bedroom of the Glessner House, Chicago, c.1887. Furnishings used included textiles by Morris & Co. and Thomas Wardle.

47. George Walton: the drawing room fireplace of a house in Brasted, Kent, with stencilled canvas walls and specially woven Morton carpets.

48. 'A simple room' in London, with blue and green upholstery and hangings. From the American publication *The Craftsman*, 1904.

The division of wall space had changed considerably from the 1870s when four distinct areas of decoration were offered. The central dado was eliminated. Instead there was a deep panel from skirting board to picture rail, with a narrow border above. As well as wallpaper, 47,86 stencilled canvas and embroidered panels were used for both areas. Stencilling suited the designs of the period beautifully and it can be said that the technique itself had a marked influence on the appearance of textiles for a few years. Green and Abbot of Oxford Street first took commercial advantage of stencilled fabrics with a range of designs by Arthur Gwatkin which they patented in 1897.[19] Hayward and Sons followed some months later with examples in watercolour on jute and silk grounds.[20] An interesting experimental works specializing in stencilled canvas was started by F. Hargreaves Smith and described in

49. The drawing room, Bailrigg, Lancaster, in 1902: a typical middle-class interior using fashionable furnishings without thought for their overall effect.

53

The Artist for 1898. Hargreaves Smith explained not only that he appreciated the challenge the technique gave to him and his assistants but that in his view 'it is the idea of individuality in treatment by the worker himself that we are especially desirous of bringing into play in the industry'.[21] It was established manufacturers, however, who had greatest success with the technique and G. P. & J. Baker provided a range of designs by Lindsay P. Butterfield which were described as 'a successful attempt to give a really marketable value to stencilled fabrics'.[22]

Around the turn of the century several manufacturers and workshops attempted to reproduce stencilled effects by other means. Batik resist or 'stencilling with wax'[23] was tried but only Dutch designers used this successfully for furnishings. 'Rainbow printing', which 9,16 resulted in shaded colours, was introduced by Turnbull and Stockdale and G. P. & J. Baker, while A. H. Lee perfected their techniques of warp-printing and of applying 117 additional colours by block onto their patterned woven fabrics.

Appliqué embroidery provided a flat silhouette effect similar to that of stencilling and became one of the most widely used techniques. It was likened to stained glass, the outline couching threads corresponding to the lead lines,[24] a theory which has some credibility when considering embroideries done by Glasgow designers who also produced stained glass 42 panels. Godfrey Blount helped to popularize appliqué techniques and elements of a similar 58,59 flat style can be seen in the hand-woven rugs and hangings made at Haslemere under Joseph King.

The importance of hand-made textiles at this time is undeniable though they formed only a small part of British factory and workshop production. The revival of traditional techniques which occurred – spinning, lace making, dyeing and hand weaving – was supremely important to the development of later twentieth-century crafts. These methods formed the foundation for all art education from primary to art school levels. However, although these articles were shown in abundance at the Arts and Crafts Exhibitions few actually reached the general market or were made in large enough quantities to have survived beyond the examples retained by the makers.

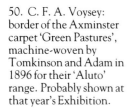

50. C. F. A. Voysey: border of the Axminster carpet 'Green Pastures', machine-woven by Tomkinson and Adam in 1896 for their 'Aluto' range. Probably shown at that year's Exhibition.

51. The sitting room of the Hotel
Metropole, Folkestone, in 1897: a cosy
yet artistic interior by the London firm
of Smee & Cobay. The armchairs are
upholstered with a Voysey fabric (see
Ill. 52).

52. C. F. A. Voysey: pattern
incorporating seagulls, woven by
Alexander Morton & Co., c. 1896.
This is the fabric used for upholstery
at the Hotel Metropole (Ill. 51).

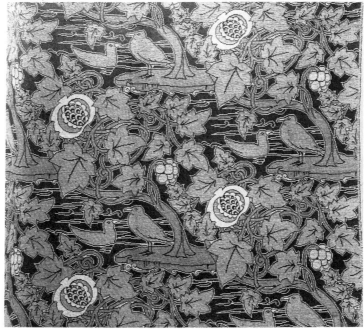

Colour plates

53. C. F. A. Voysey: jacquard-woven woollen double cloth manufactured by Alexander Morton & Co. The design, originally conceived as a wallpaper c. 1896, was also used in this form and as a gauze.

54. C. F. A. Voysey: 'Seagulls', watercolour and pencil design, 1890-91. This was produced as a silk and wool fabric by Alexander Morton & Co. and shown at the 1893 Exhibition.

55. C. F. A. Voysey: watercolour and pencil design, c. 1893, used as a wallpaper ('The Minstrel') and as a woven woollen fabric ('The Pilgrim') by Alexander Morton & Co.

56. C. F. A. Voysey: watercolour design for a printed fabric, c. 1888. The design was bought by G. P. & J. Baker and produced as a velveteen and a printed silk (see Ill. 57).

57. C. F. A. Voysey: block-printed silk bedcover produced by G. P. & J. Baker c. 1895, using Voysey's design of c. 1888 (see Ill. 56). Probably sold through Liberty's.

58. Godfrey Blount: appliqué panel of hand-woven linen embroidered by the Haslemere Peasant Industries, 1896-7.

59. Godfrey Blount: 'The Spies', appliqué panel of hand-woven linen embroidered by the Haslemere Peasant Industries, c. 1900.

60. Century Guild (A. H. Mackmurdo): 'Cromer Bird', block-printed cotton manufactured by Simpson & Godlee, c. 1884.

61. Century Guild (A. H. Mackmurdo): wool and cotton hanging woven by A. H. Lee & Sons, 1887-8. This was probably shown at the first Arts and Crafts Exhibition.

62. Lewis F. Day: 'The New Dot', indigo discharge and block-printed cotton manufactured by Turnbull and Stockdale in 1898. In this process the cotton is first dipped into the indigo vat, producing an even blue ground; it is then printed with a bleaching agent; and finally the surplus dye is cleared away, leaving the design in white, or pale blue if a weaker bleach was used.

54

55

56

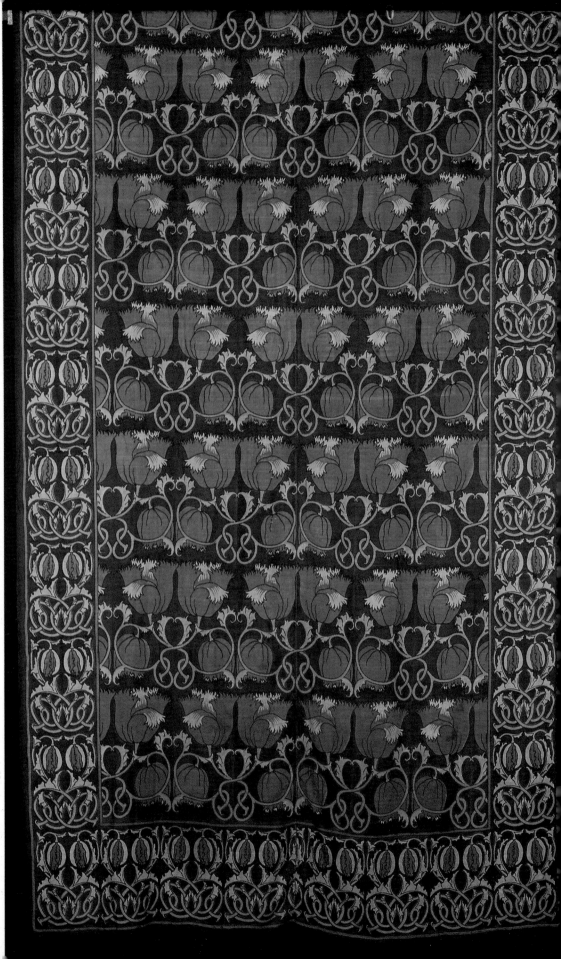

57

CONFORTAMINI ET AFFERTE
NOBIS DE FRVCTIBVS TERRÆ

58

62

3 Textiles in the Arts and Crafts Exhibitions

HE catalogues of the Arts and Crafts Society's Exhibitions are not illustrated and as the information they contain tends to be vague and often misleading, it is necessary to study contemporary press reports to discover exactly what was exhibited and which pieces caught public attention.

Magazine articles provide a fascinating gauge of the times: what started out as scant cover for the Society's first exhibition in 1888 reached a high point of interest and enthusiasm in 1903. Most of the early reviews concentrate on a few items, and although this does have the advantage of identifying the most eye-catching pieces, these were not necessarily the most significant. One can detect that selection has often been made on grounds of size, dominance in display, quaintness or eccentricity, but such frailties of human nature are, in themselves, informative. Furnishing magazines tended to restrict their remarks to the suitability of objects for the trade, which was a limiting view on a Society based on a strong artistic philosophy. One magazine dismissed most of the applied arts in the 1896 Exhibition as 'of the neo-Medieval or pseudo-Florentine type' (which was untrue) and in the same year totally missed the significance of Charles Rennie Mackintosh's first exhibit, a settle with a stencilled canvas back. Describing this piece of furniture as 'upholstered meagrely . . . by means of simple and unpretending tin tacks', the article went on to suggest that the Society 'expunge this "Uriah Heap" sentiment from the production of the Brotherhood'.[1]

The Studio, started by Gleeson White in 1893, set a new trend for it was in full accord with the aims of the Society and published lengthy and sensitive reviews of the exhibitions. Moreover, for the first time textiles were covered in as much detail as the other arts. This unusual interest was ridiculed in established art journals and, following the remark in *The Studio* that the magazine felt it a 'greater service to develop beautiful textiles than classical gods and goddesses',[2] the August 1894 issue of *The Artist* published a scathing poem under the title 'Doctor Textiles' which included the following doggerel:

> Now let Great Britain all rejoice
> (And also let the next isles)
> Since the good *Studio* casting voice
> Gives up the Gods for textiles.
>
> The new aesthete will dote on stoves,
> Seek fire-dogs and annex tiles,
> Indoors in future are his loves,
> For there he keeps his textiles.

Art-counterpane and vallance will
Spread peace through all these vexed isles,
And art will concentrate her skill
On 'beautiful textiles'.

As many hundreds of textiles were exhibited at the eleven Arts and Crafts Exhibitions covered by this study,[3] it is sensible to examine these in three chronological groups, each of which shows distinctive artistic and technical developments.

1888-1890

Before the first exhibition at the New Gallery in October 1888 the Selection Committee of the Arts and Crafts Society[4] had written to all members of the Art Workers' Guild as well as to a number of firms associated with decorative work inviting them to submit objects for possible selection. It was rare, however, for manufacturers not to be able to buy their way into an exhibition and to control the space that they could use.[5] The insistence by the Society on full recognition in the labelling and catalogue being given to all designers, manufacturers and executants further contributed to a dearth of commercially produced textiles in the first few exhibitions. Of the seventy-one textile-related exhibits in 1888 (including seven designs), only four firms were represented, giving an indication of the intransigent attitude of some and secretiveness of others, afraid of poaching by competitors. Three of the firms were Templeton & Co. of Glasgow, Morris & Co. and Turnbull and Stockdale. The fourth manufacturer, Thomas Wardle, more than made up for the restricted size of this commercial section, showing a collection of printed silks, cretonnes, 21,64 velvets, linens, challis, silk damasks and silk plushes. It would appear that he himself broke the rules, as the catalogue entry for these fabrics simply describes them as 'Colourings by Thomas Wardle'.[6]

With the exception of Turnbull's roller-printed cottons and Templeton's machine- 14,105 woven carpets, all the other textiles displayed (tapestries, carpets, woven and printed fabrics, lace and embroidery) were hand-made. This imbalance in the display has led to the impression that all Arts and Crafts textiles were made at home or in small workshops. This was not the case, despite embroideries accounting for by far the largest element in the textile sections at any of the exhibitions. The *Art Journal* was quick to deplore the state of affairs which 'showed too much evidence of the hand of a single gentlewoman with a mission'.[7] Yet, however uneven in numbers, it is the mixing of mass-produced commercial exhibits with individually designed and worked items that is one of the most significant elements of the Society's exhibitions. This was to encourage a totally different attitude to textile production in the twentieth century.

The comparative inexperience of the Society's Selection Committee is shown in the first three exhibitions, which reflected a hesitancy in choice and a wide range of styles. This was understandable for a group in search of a definite identity but the juxtaposition of some exhibits must have looked particularly odd. In 1888 the Royal Windsor Tapestry Company, a bastion of the establishment, exhibited the Herbert Bone cartoon and tapestry,

63. Century Guild (A. H. Mackmurdo): wooden screen made by Wilkinson & Sons with panels embroidered in silks and Japanese gold thread. Shown at the 1888 Exhibition.

'King Arthur in the Danish Camp', and these were shown with three Morris & Co. panels, 37 'St Cecilia', 'The Woodpecker' and 'The Forest', belonging to a totally different aesthetic world. The Royal Windsor Tapestry Company never again took part in an Arts and Crafts Exhibition.

Other exhibits in 1888 included three designs by Voysey for printed textiles (without noticeable comment from the press) and two printed cottons by Sidney Mawson. The 34,61 Century Guild were represented by hangings, hand-painted satins, a pile rug and an embroidered screen designed by Mackmurdo and made by Wilkinson & Sons of Old Bond 63 Street. These items were the last that the group displayed publicly, as they disbanded the same year.[8]

Forty-five different embroideries were shown, from large *portières* to panels, cabinets, screens, curtains, bedcovers, piano covers, altar frontals, book covers, picture frames and borders. They were submitted by various groups and individuals, notably the Leek Embroidery Society, the Decorative Needlework Society, the Donegal Industrial Fund, Jane, Jenny and May Morris, Catherine Holiday, Una Taylor, Mary Buckle and Mrs J. Aldam Heaton, the wife of the furnisher. Of all the embroideries exhibited, Mrs Walter Crane's mantel valance worked in white cotton on black wool was singled out for praise by several journals.

Many of the women exhibiting textiles are known only by the names of their husbands who provided the designs for their work. While this would seem unfair, since success was equally dependent on their skills, it must be remembered that the exhibitions gave women the first opportunity to appear alongside men on equal terms and that these were the titles they elected to be known by when submitting their exhibits. This social formality was not always followed, and Catherine Holiday, for example, who was already a professional embroideress of over ten years' standing, was listed with her own Christian name, as was Phoebe Traquair, together with other outstanding single craftswomen such as Una Taylor, Mary Buckle, Mary Gemmell and Mary Newill, who all received personal recognition.

The artistic and financial success of the 1888 Exhibition[9] encouraged the Society to arrange another, one year later, in enlarged accommodation in the New Gallery. The public were now accustomed to this new kind of show and it became a significant London event.

Of 221 textiles exhibited in 1889, 91 were embroideries, and the exhibition was marked by a notable increase in items submitted by Morris & Co., indicating Morris's own acceptance of the success of the Society after earlier misgivings.[10] Voysey and Day both submitted designs for printed fabrics and Turnbull and Stockdale showed some of Day's block- and roller-printed onto cotton. Thomas Wardle exhibited numerous printed fabrics with Eastern-inspired patterns as well as some original designs, this time acknowledging their creators. *The Artist* for 1 December 1889 described this work as 'splendidly sumptuous, 64 glowing dyes of the richest hues being used with masterly purpose to a worthy end'.

Most of the embroideresses represented in 1888 submitted work again and *The Artist* commented that the many embroideries 'dazzle by their beauty and appal by their quantity'. Among the new exhibitors were Mrs H. S. Ashbee[11] and Mrs George Jack. Organizations included the Langdale Linen Industry in the Lake District (a frequent exhibitor at the Home Arts and Industries Exhibitions) and two London shops, Maison Helbronner and Jonathan Harris. The latter commissioned the Royal School of Art Needlework to embroider a chair back using linen from their own factory at Cockermouth in the Lake District.

The increasing confidence of the Society as an exhibiting body and of the artists, craftsmen and designers as contributors is clear to see in the variety and range of objects included in the 1889 catalogue. Like William Morris, the previously doubting press were forced to admit that the exhibitions had met with some success. The *Illustrated London*

64. Block-printed silk designed by Mrs T. S. Coombe for Thomas Wardle. Shown at the 1888 Exhibition as a velveteen, and in 1889 as a silk.

News found 'sufficient evidence that the ideas put forward by the Committee had met with ready reception by an increasing body of employers and workmen'.[12]

The original aim that the exhibitions should be held every year was followed at the end of 1890 with a third show, but this proved to be a financial disaster and the Society never again held exhibitions at such short intervals. The decision by the Committee to concentrate on embroidery and furniture was particularly misguided, with 120 examples of needlework swamping the textile section. The catalogue indicates that much of the vitality and originality of the two previous shows was missing since not enough new work was available. In retrospect, however, a few important exhibits stand out. Arthur Silver showed two designs, William Morris's favourite embroideress, Catherine Holiday, displayed two embroidered hangings (one designed by Morris), and the first embroideries designed by Lewis F. Day and worked by Mary Buckle appeared.[13] Another notable exhibit, which showed the strong political views of many members of the Society, was an Irish National Banner designed by Walter Crane, embroidered by Una Taylor and signed by Charles Stewart Parnell. This caused none of the controversy that would greet the public display of such an object today.

At the close of the exhibition the Society's accounts showed a deficit of £138.19s.1d. Despite this and low attendances,[14] the press saw beyond what was a temporary setback. 'The periodic displays are fast gaining general recognition as illustrations of a real movement and as evidences of a new development of artistic opinion . . . Before long if we may judge from the signs, the Arts and Crafts Society will have a large following drawn from the ranks of the outside and unprofessional public', wrote *The Artist* for 1 November 1890. One of the main successes of the Society was the encouragement of visits by members of the public who were unused to attending exhibitions, artisans in particular. The Committee had done this by attempting to keep entrance fees low,[15] and by opening in the evenings and, occasionally, on Sundays. They had also organized a series of public lectures covering all aspects of the arts displayed.[16]

65. The artist-craftsman symbol of the Arts and Crafts Exhibition Society, used on a 1903 season ticket.

1893-1903

The decision by the Arts and Crafts Society to wait just over two years for their next exhibition was a wise one. They had proved that their aims were not far-fetched and, with a decent interval of time, enough new material became available to make a display worthwhile. They were also able to repay members who had acted as guarantors and had forfeited money over the losses of 1890.[17]

The decade 1893-1903 proved to be the most significant period in the development of textiles of the Arts and Crafts Movement. Not only did a very original style evolve but the range of patterns and techniques used in industry and at home showed a level of sophistication not seen since the eighteenth century. Although the exhibitions were never able to display a representative selection of commercial textiles they did give some indication of this new successful phase.

In 1893 the more traditional exhibits such as Morris tapestries and carpets (including
66 their finest, 'The Bullerswood') were joined for the first time by designs by Butterfield, John Scarratt Rigby and John Illingworth Kay. Thomas Wardle exhibited three of his finest
67,36 printed fabrics, designed by his son Thomas Wardle, Jr, Léon Victor Solon, and Walter Crane.[18] Crane also supplied the most illustrated exhibit of the year, a design for a damask
68 tablecloth called 'The Senses'. With this John Wilson exhibited the finished cloth, which was later described by Day as a 'tour-de-force in damask'.[19] This piece demonstrated both a renewed interest in the technique by the leading artists of the day and the use of modern design by one of the most conservative of all the traditional industries.

There were fewer embroideries in 1893 but they indicated a general improvement in
80 standards. Mrs Jack produced a charming copy of a Rossetti engraving, which contrasted beautifully with more professionally worked items such as a set of curtains designed by May
81 Morris for her father's bed at Kelmscott Manor and embroidered by her and other Morris & Co. employees. Mary Newill, the Birmingham designer and craftswoman, exhibited for the first time, while the Royal School of Art Needlework, the Langdale Linen Industry and the Leek Embroidery Society continued to be represented.

The death of William Morris on 3 October 1896, the proposed opening day of the fifth Arts and Crafts Exhibition, delayed its start and, quite understandably, monopolized the first press reviews, with *The Studio* referring mawkishly to 'a splendid moment for a hero to die'.[20] The news had come too late for any special arrangements to be made to honour Morris (these were to come later) and the exhibition proceeded as planned. It was to prove the most influential and forward-looking of all, with participation from three of the most progressive art schools of the day – Birmingham, Liverpool and Glasgow – including, for
69 the first time, examples of work by ex-Glasgow School of Art students whose influence on European design was to have profound effects in the years to come. Little of the significance of these exhibits is discernible in the art magazines, which gave more attention to regular exhibitors. One interesting development that was commented upon was the opportunity for each artist to experiment 'in branches of Art in which he is not expert':[21] the painters John Batten, Henry Holiday and Heywood Sumner (best known for his sgraffito work) were all represented by embroidery designs. The Batten panel, worked by Agnes Day, is particularly notable technically since it has additional small painted ivory details.

Exhibits in 1893

66. William Morris and J. H. Dearle: 'The Bullerswood', hand-knotted carpet, woven in wool on a cotton warp in 1889.

67. Thomas Wardle, Jr:
'Crown Imperial', block-
printed cotton manufac-
tured and registered by
Thomas Wardle in
December 1893. Sold
through Heal's at 2s. a
yard.

68. Walter Crane: 'The
Senses', watercolour
design for a linen damask
tablecloth woven by John
Wilson & Sons. It was
exhibited with the finished
cloth (now in the V&A).

69. C. R. Mackintosh: wooden settle with stencilled canvas back.

70. C. F. A. Voysey: 'The Fairyland', woollen fabric woven by Alexander Morton & Co.

71. C. F. A. Voysey: Wilton carpet machine-woven by Tomkinson and Adam for Liberty's.

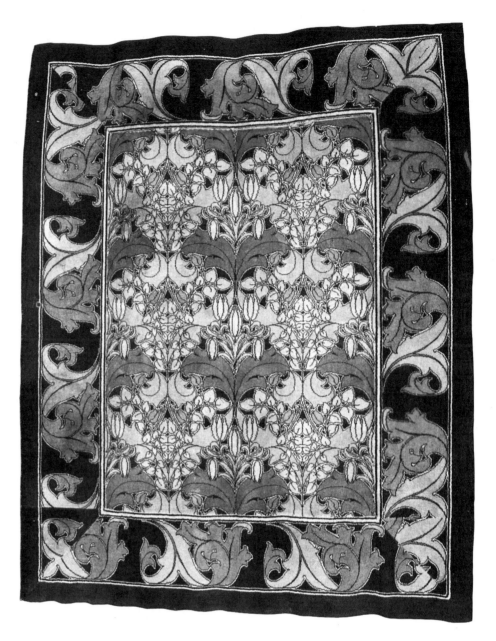

Commercial textile manufacture was represented both by well established firms and by a number of new designers. There were printed cottons and velveteens from Turnbull and Stockdale and Thomas Wardle and woven fabrics from the Society's two leading manufac-
70 turers in this field, Alexander Morton and A. H. Lee. Lee exhibited woollens from designs by G. F. Armitage and Samuel Rowe, and, for the first time, Alexander Morton (who had previously exhibited a gauze and a heavy woollen cloth) showed the very attractive silk and wool cloths for which he later became famous.
50,71   Voysey, Butterfield, Gavin Morton and Arthur Silver showed designs either on paper or as fabrics. Silver exhibited a design called 'Peacock', continuing his use of this bird as a
15 subject for printed fabrics, which included his 'Peacock Feather' for Liberty's in 1888. Three new textile designers also appeared in 1896 – Edgar Pattison, Sidney Haward and George R. Rigby. Pattison and Haward are chiefly known for traditional patterns (one of

Pattison's designs in 1896 was for the by then old-fashioned 'chintz') whereas George Rigby's style is characterized by the fashionable flat pastel effects achieved by stencilling, 91 influenced, no doubt, by his activities as an illustrator and designer of wallpapers and friezes. The most original ideas for textiles came from Scotland. Charles Rennie Mackintosh designed a settle made by J. & W. Guthrie, and the relatively unknown embroideress 69 Jessie Newbery exhibited work made to her designs by students of her embroidery classes at the Glasgow School of Art. She had shown an altar frontal in 1893; but these secular pieces, more suited to her style, were a coverlet worked by Mary Rowat and two cushion covers and a mantle border embroidered by Jenny Rowat, Edith Rowat[22] and Jessie Cleland. She exhibited only once more at the London Arts and Crafts Exhibitions, in 1899, thereafter concentrating on her teaching. Her methods, in which silk embroidery was 82,85 worked onto linen in unusual linear designs, were continued by one of her best students and her eventual successor, Ann Macbeth, who showed at the Arts and Crafts Exhibitions of 32,33, 1903, 1906 and 1916. European interest in Glasgow design was aroused by the early work of 83 Mackintosh, Margaret and Frances Macdonald and Jessie Newbery at exhibitions such as 42,69 these and was consolidated by the exhibitions at Glasgow in 1901 and Turin in 1902.

The growing importance of British design on the Continent was becoming evident both from foreign press coverage of the Arts and Crafts Exhibitions and from the number of requests for the Society to organize exhibitions abroad.[23] It is significant that in 1896 Hermann Obrist, one of the most progressive Continental designers, chose to exhibit six examples worked in his Munich embroidery *atelier*. There was also increasing interest from foreign buyers. Manufacturers wanted to purchase British designs, and British-made goods, particularly textiles, were ordered by fashionable shops including Bing's Maison de l'Art 133 Nouveau in Paris, Von Burchard Sohne and Hirschwald's Hohenzollern Kaufhaus in Berlin, Von Braes in Düsseldorf, Walther's in Frankfurt-am-Main, Robert Furtwängler in 115 Zurich, Erik Folcker's Sub Rosa in Stockholm, Steen & Strøm in Christiania (Oslo), and Konstantin-Hansen & Bindesbøll in Copenhagen. The *Magazine of Art* maintained, quite rightly, that the exhibitions had helped to bring British decorative arts 'to the front rank, if not the head of all nations'.[24] With such widespread recognition the Arts and Crafts Movement was finally born.

The decision to hold a William Morris retrospective section in the 1899 Exhibition was taken more from sentiment than practicality. Morris's influence on and value to the Society had been incalculable but a large repetitive display of his work, which now looked rather old-fashioned, was not the way for a modern, vigorous and optimistic organization to mark its respect, nor was it what he would have wanted himself. The Society was always at its best when looking ahead and only in 1912 and 1916, both significant years in its decline, did it again look back.

The 1899 and 1903 Exhibitions showed an increase in hand weaving and in other revived traditional industries such as Honiton lace and Donegal carpet making. The embroidery section was dominated by professional women who, with the confidence that past successes in the exhibitions had given, began to show work which they had designed as well as embroidered. May Morris, Mary Newill, Una Taylor and Phoebe Traquair were the 72,73 most important, although Una Taylor's most famous works today are those designed by 75,76 others. Two of the best nineteenth-century sets of pictorial embroideries were displayed at

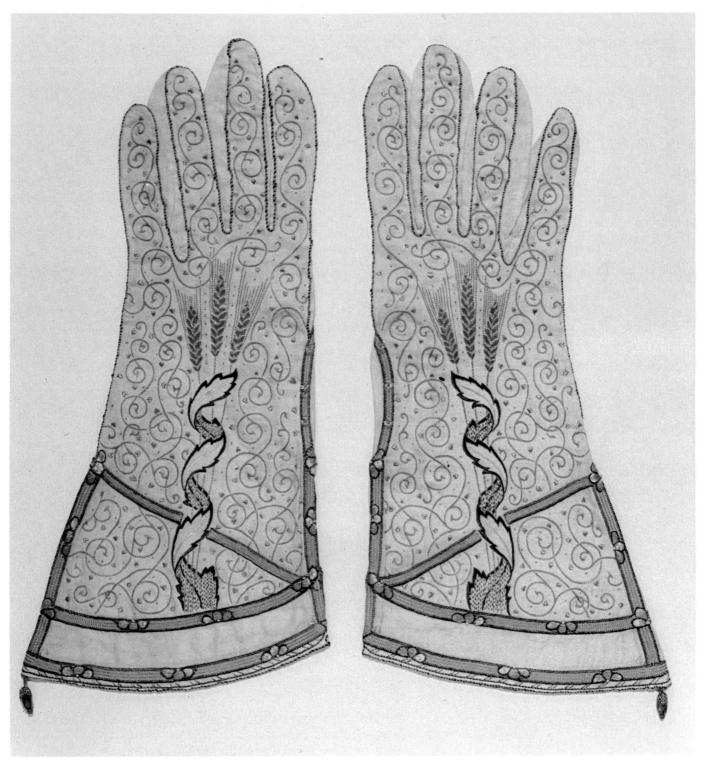

72. Bishop's gloves, designed by Charles Ricketts and embroidered in silks on linen by May Morris. Shown at the 1899 Exhibition.

73. The dining room in 'Top o' the Hill', 1900, showing two of the *Faerie Queene* panels designed by Mary Newill and made by the Bromsgrove Guild. The embroideries were shown at the 1899 Exhibition, and again in Paris in 1900.

74. Mary Newill: panel from a set of embroideries illustrating the *Faerie Queene*, a variation of those for Edmund Butler (Ill. 73).

this time. In 1899 Mary Newill exhibited her finest work, a set of appliqué panels based on 73 Spenser's *Faerie Queene* made by the Bromsgrove Guild of Applied Arts, an organization set up by past students of the Birmingham School of Art. They perfectly suited the room for which they were designed in Edmund Butler's house, 'Top o' the Hill', in Sutton Coldfield. Phoebe Traquair's narrative panels, sometimes called 'The Story of Genius', were given a 75,76 prime spot in 1903 at the end of the West Gallery. Based on Walter Pater's *Imaginary Portraits*, these four embroideries were worked between 1895 and 1902 in a variety of stitches which cover the entire ground.

The 1903 Exhibition is significant not only because of the new kinds of objects shown but also because of the manner in which they were displayed. Earlier mishaps with textiles (one coverlet was nailed to a wall, another lost) had prompted inhibiting rules including the framing of smaller objects not in cases and regulation sizes for repeating designs.[25] The

75, 76. (*opposite*) Phoebe Traquair: the first and third panels from a set of four embroideries, 'The Story of Genius', worked in silks and gold thread on linen. The set was shown at the 1903 Exhibition and priced at £1,000.

overall effect must have been improved by the decoration of the gallery, with white painted canvas covered walls and standard bay trees in tubs.[26] The canvas made an ideal background, especially for Morton's shot silk and wool fabrics (after designs by Voysey and Butterfield) and for the fresh, light-coloured, floral patterns exhibited by Cecil Millar and 89 Allan Vigers. It was also a suitably textured contrast for the hand-woven textiles, which 27 included work by Luther Hooper of Haslemere, Annie Garnett of Windermere, and Grace Christie, who showed embroideries as well as small hand-woven tapestries.

Colour plates

77. M. H. Baillie Scott: watercolour design for the bedroom of a country cottage, 1902. This shows the architect's keen interest in furnishing textiles, particularly printed fabrics and appliqué embroidery.

78. M. H. Baillie Scott: detail of a panel from a screen, silk appliqué on a cotton and hemp ground embroidered by Mrs Scott. This was shown at the 1896 Exhibition.

79. May Morris: 'The Orchard', wall hanging embroidered in silks on a silk ground, 1896. Another version of this design was called 'The Fruit Garden'.

80. Mrs George Jack (Annie Gray): embroidered picture in silks on linen based on an engraving by Dante Gabriel Rossetti. This was shown at the 1893 Exhibition.

81. William Morris's bed at Kelmscott Manor, with hangings and cover designed by May Morris. The bedcover was embroidered by Jane Morris; the hangings (which were shown at the 1893 Exhibition) by May assisted by Lily Yeats and Ellen Wright.

82. Jessie Newbery: linen appliqué cushion cover embroidered in silks with edges of needleweaving, worked by the designer, c. 1900.

83. Ann Macbeth: detail of a linen tablecloth with linen appliqué and silk embroidery, worked by the designer, c. 1900.

84. Charles Rennie Mackintosh: watercolour design on tracing paper for a printed or embroidered textile border, c. 1900.

85. Jessie Newbery: linen collar embroidered in silks with bead decoration, worked by the designer, c. 1900.

86. George Walton: stencilled linen frieze, c. 1903. This may be the one shown at the 1906 Exhibition.

87. Harry Napper: 'Waterlilies', watercolour design for a block-printed fabric manufactured by G. P. & J. Baker in 1905. Baker's bought designs from Napper after he left the Silver Studio.

88. Harry Napper: 'Magnolia Tree', watercolour design for a roller-printed fabric manufactured by G. P. & J. Baker in 1906. The fabric was sold through Liberty's and also used by them for upholstery.

89. Cecil Millar: 'Pansy', watercolour design for a block-printed linen manufactured by G. P. & J. Baker in 1903, and probably shown by the manufacturers at the 1903 Exhibition. A number of Millar's designs were sold through Heal's in the early twentieth century.

90. Harry Napper: silk and wool fabric woven by J. W. & C. Ward of Halifax, c. 1900. The design shows elements of the work of Voysey and was, until recently, attributed to him.

91. George Rigby: 'Japanese Rose', watercolour design for a block-printed fabric manufactured by G. P. & J. Baker in 1902.

92. John Scarratt Rigby: block-printed silk tablecloth or bedcover manufactured by G. P. & J. Baker, probably the same as that listed as 'Ragged Poppy' in the firm's records for 1902.

77

78

79

80

the winds, on the wold / and the night is a cold / and thames runs chill
twixt mead & hill / but kind & dear / is the old house here
and my heart is warm / midst winter's harm / rest then & rest : and think
of the best / twixt summer & spring / when all birds sing
in the town of the tree / and ye in me / and scarce the
more let earth & love / old tale away

82

83

84

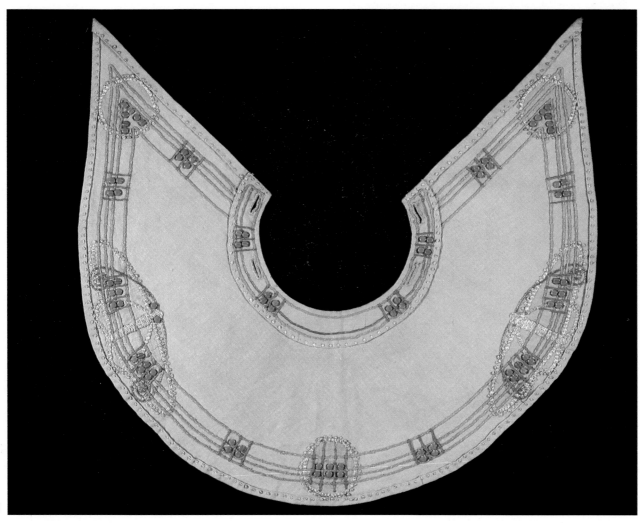

85

86

87

88

89

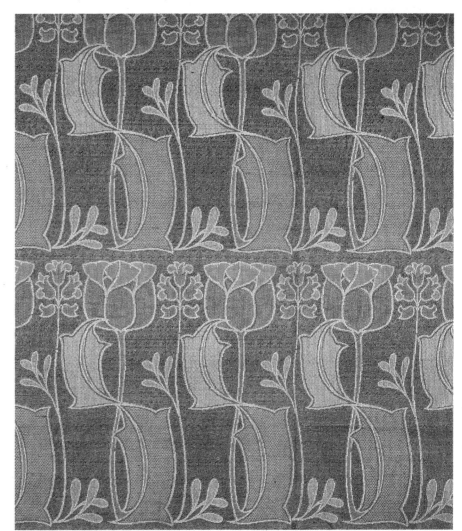

90

91

1906-1916

Various organizational problems beset the Committee after the turn of the century and the four exhibitions between 1906 and 1916 were each held at a different venue: the Grafton Gallery in 1906,[27] the New Gallery for the last time in 1910,[28] the Grosvenor Gallery in 1912, and, as an ironic finishing point to this study, the Royal Academy in 1916.

The standard of commercial exhibits declined considerably from 1906 onwards and few examples show either the originality in design or the quality of the textiles which were produced on the Continent, especially in Austria and Germany. The exhibitions were accused of not keeping pace with the best British work available. 'There is more than one tradesman in London today who . . . could make a far better and more artistic display of British craftsmanship than is to be seen at the Grafton Gallery', *The Studio* wrote of the 1906 Exhibition.[29] The embroideress Ann Macbeth continued to participate; the absence of other members of the Glasgow School was blamed on the Selection Committee, although it is not known how many items they submitted. They are likely to have been preoccupied with more influential international exhibitions.

The number of preparatory designs and printed textiles diminished and patterns were mostly interchangeable (for use as wallpapers or fabrics), with a marked preference for historical motifs. The most frequent exhibitors – Cecil Millar, Lewis F. Day, Sidney Mawson, Alfred Carpenter, Edgar Pattison and Joseph Doran – were very successful designers because they worked in several styles and were able, therefore, to satisfy almost all sections of the trade. A favourite pattern both for roller-printed and for power-loom-woven fabrics was taken from seventeenth-century crewelwork embroideries. Day, Mawson, Millar and Frederick Vigers all produced straight reproductions of these hangings for A. H. Lee and for the printers Foxton's, Turnbull and Stockdale, and Thomas Wardle.

Only a few glimmers of past glories were seen in the later exhibitions. George Walton's stencilled linen frieze shown in 1906 and his carpets woven by Alexander Morton and exhibited in 1910 typified the best developments in British design during these years, combining the most original elements from home and abroad.

With the exception of the exhibits described above, the textile sections in the last four Arts and Crafts Exhibitions were dominated by the revival of hand-loom weaving, which grew from eight examples in 1906 to a staggering sixty-three in 1916, in a great variety of styles. The increasing interest in the craft had been noticed at the beginning of the century by Mabel Cox, who, writing about the 1900 Home Arts and Industries Exhibition, commented on the numbers of moderately priced, beautifully coloured and imaginatively textured examples shown. She concluded that 'On the whole, spinning and weaving may safely be said to be the most useful and most artistically valuable of the revived industries.'[30] From this time fabric structure and texture took over from surface pattern with the greater use of draft, heddle and simple frame looms. Technique controlled design.

Morris & Co. attempted to find new markets by showing again their hand-jacquard fabrics seen in previous exhibitions. During the firm's years of financial crisis, H. C. Marillier and J. H. Dearle, the company's Managing and Artistic Directors, were sensible in looking for influential public displays for their newly woven tapestries: in 1910 they

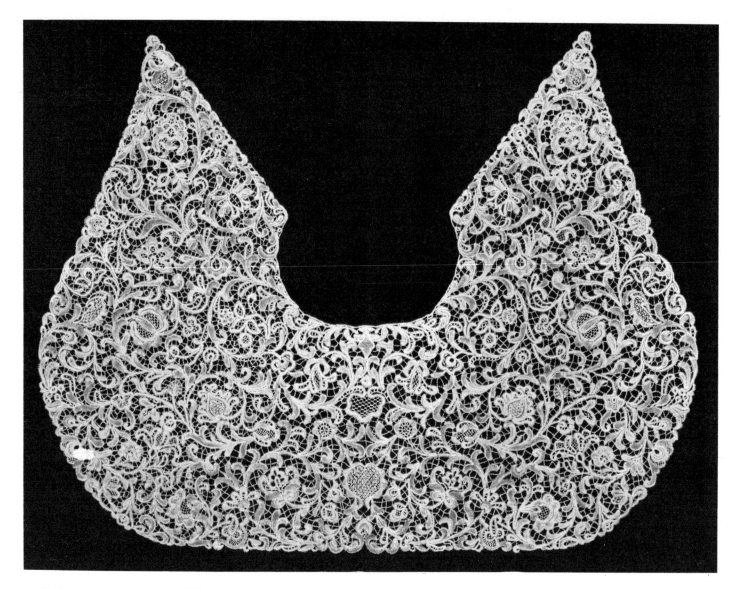

93. Lewis F. Day: Honiton lace collar, possibly the one shown at the 1910 Exhibition, worked by members of the East Devon Cottage Lace Industry.

94. Alfred Carpenter: 'The Jay', roller-printed cotton by Turnbull and Stockdale. Shown at the 1910 Exhibition.

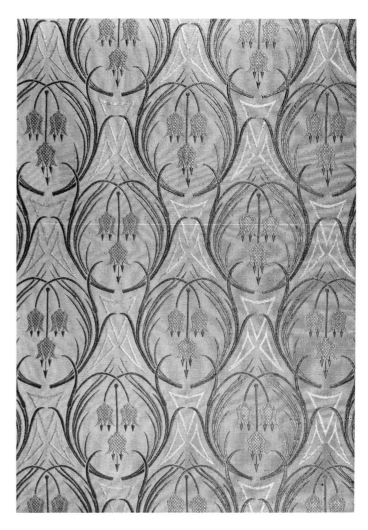

showed designs by Byam Shaw, Heywood Sumner and Dearle himself, and in 1912 a panel by Mrs Adrian Stokes. Edmund Hunter, one of the most influential weavers of the new school and founder of the St Edmundsbury Weavers, exhibited his first piece, a hand-tufted rug, in 1906. In 1912 he displayed eight fabrics and in 1916 nine examples woven in natural fibres – wool, cotton, silk and linen – and some with metal thread. The revival of old structures and the experimental use of metals and, later, synthetic yarns was evident in a number of exhibits. Annie Garnett produced an intriguingly named 'samite' (a medieval fabric) in her workshop in Windermere and Katie Grasett, the London weaver, showed cloth woven from a mixture of silk, gold and aluminium in 1912 and 1916. Other notable exhibitors in 1916 included Jean Milne and Ethel Mairet who provided ten items, among them a jerkin of hand-spun, indigo-dyed and hand-woven cloth.

By 1912 there was a general feeling voiced through the press that the Society had completed its mission. There had been a marked decline in the standards of amateur work and the rather mundane application of embroidery, in particular, provoked repeated

95. Edmund Hunter: 'Vineyard', silk tissue, c.1905, woven by the St Edmundsbury Weavers and shown at the 1912 Exhibition.

96. Annie Garnett: 'Fritillary', hand-loom-woven silk manufactured at the Spinnery, Windermere, c.1900-1910.

97. The Textile Room, 1916. The Christine Angus dalmatic (Ill.98) can be seen at the side in the central glass case.

comments. Elaborate pictures were now unfashionable and the technique was used almost exclusively for the decoration of domestic items. Catalogues list table linen, tea cloths, bags, collars, pockets, children's dresses and other costume accessories worked, for the most part, by women known only from single embroideries.

The last two exhibitions saw not only the passing of an artistic phase but also the deaths of two of the most famous designers associated with the Society. Lewis F. Day died in April 1910 and a tribute by Walter Crane was published in the introductory notes to the 1912 catalogue. In March 1915 Crane himself died. The Presidency of the Society and responsibility for organizing the 1916 Exhibition were undertaken by Henry Wilson, the Birmingham metalworker. The last exhibition was large (over twice the number of exhibits seen in 1888) and probably more ambitious than any before. There were retrospective sections containing the work of D. G. Rossetti, Ford Madox Brown, Edward Burne-Jones and Morris and a hint of nostalgia in alcoves devoted to works shown in past Arts and Crafts Exhibitions. There were some new textiles as well but, on the whole, this section was 97,98 indicative of the confused state of British design, forced to turn in upon itself after two years of devastating world war. As founder, chief supporter and long-standing President, Walter Crane's organizing flair was sadly missed, and with his passing the Society's exhibitions never recovered their vitality or relevance to modern design and manufacture.

98. Christine Angus: dalmatic for a
children's service, shown at the 1916
Exhibition. (The silk embroidered
panels, originally on silk damask as seen
here, have since been re-applied to
velvet.)

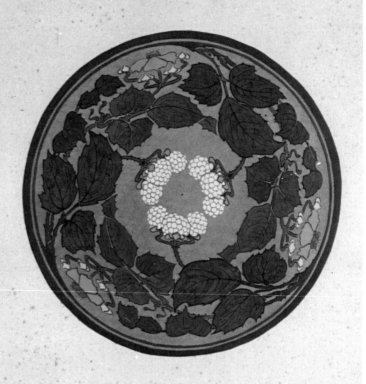

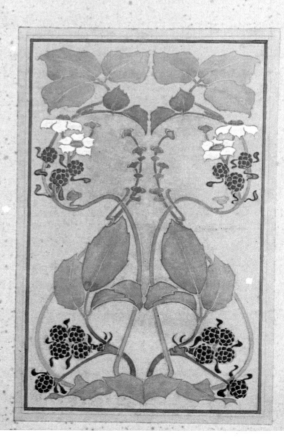

4 Designers, Manufacturers and Shops

HE training of future designers began at last to meet the needs of industry and of a new, artistically aware, public. A radical improvement in draughtsmanship followed the involvement of architects. Moreover, art schools began to understand commercial realities and reflected this knowledge in their teaching. The National Competition of Schools of Science and Art and Art Classes held in South Kensington bore witness to these improvements. Open to art students throughout Great Britain, it provided an incentive for them to compete with one another, win prizes and display their work in public. Respect for the competition is shown in the increasing numbers of entries both by individual students and by colleges in the last years of the nineteenth century: 91,293 applications were made in 1900,[1] and illustrated magazine articles show the very high standard of work achieved.

Another opportunity for young designers to publicize their work was presented by the International *Studio* Exhibition, started by the magazine in 1901. Not just restricted to British students, this proved, for a few years, to be even more influential than the National Competition, and prize-winning entries were illustrated in *The Studio* and also in foreign magazines, such as *Art et Décoration* and *Der Moderne Stil*. A number of provincial art schools became well known through these competitions and the publicity encouraged many of them to show their students' work alongside that of professional designers and manufacturers. Manchester School of Art displayed both woven and printed textiles at the Manchester Arts and Crafts Exhibitions and by 1896 the Birmingham School of Art was a regular exhibitor with the London Arts and Crafts Society.

Many of the long-established London art schools took a greater interest in the applied arts but their training did not meet contemporary needs. In 1896, however, a new school was started with the aim of providing 'instruction in those branches of design which directly bear on the more artistic trades'.[2] Called the Central School of Arts and Crafts, with premises in Regent Street, its first directors were George Frampton, the sculptor, and William Richard Lethaby, the architect. Unlike other schools of art which were under the control of the Government, through the Board of Education, the Central School was conceived and financed by London County Council and was, therefore, London's only municipal art school. It became a shining example of modern teaching methods and its recruitment of leading artists and designers as teachers was at the heart of its success. All handicrafts were given equal consideration, and the advantage of being taught by those with direct industrial experience was incalculable. The Central School's teaching of embroidery and hand weaving in the late nineteenth and early twentieth centuries became

99. An unknown student's work showing designs based on the blackberry, c.1900. It is impressed 'ESK', suggesting that it was approved by the South Kensington Examination Board.

95

legendary, as students who had attended the classes of Maggie Briggs, May Morris, Ellen Wright, Walter Taylor and Luther Hooper went on to become influential designers and craftsmen in their own right and the teachers of future generations.

The improvement in the teaching of commercial art resulted in a greater number of free-lance designers working for industry. It is interesting to note the high numbers that were able to make a living from the profession. Lindsay P. Butterfield (who had trained at the National Art Training School in South Kensington) earned £167.10s.10d. in 1892, his first year as a designer, and by 1898 had an average annual income of £400. Perhaps because it was becoming more lucrative, architects increasingly produced repeating designs as part of their normal work.

Not all commercial textiles were created by free-lance designers. *Kelly's Directory* each year continued to list a few 'pattern drawers', the kind of people who supplied anonymous working drawings with no artistic pretensions. Studio work, of one kind or another, still contributed a large proportion of the designs used commercially. Most large manufacturers maintained their own studios and the artists they employed were trained within the industry. Few original designs were drawn; many were taken from pattern books, photographs[3] and historic samples. Studios also adapted the work of free-lance designers. They modified colours and repeats and, in the case of woven textiles and carpets, they painted point-papers from which the patterns were entered into the loom. The size of these 107 studios depended greatly on the number and nature of the designs used. G. P. & J. Baker employed only a few people in the studio at their Swaisland Print Works in the late nineteenth century, as the patterns they bought from the most experienced free-lance designers needed hardly any reworking. On the other hand, some studios were very large and in 1908 Alexander Millar, in a series of articles on the carpet industry, described one firm as employing one hundred and fifty people 'putting colour upon paper in one shape or another'.[4]

The number of independent studios producing textile designs increased towards the end of the nineteenth century. The highly successful Silver Studio was established by Arthur Silver in 1880, and soon became one of the main suppliers of wallpaper and textile 100 designs to all the most fashionable manufacturers and shops. It also contributed directly to 114 the reputation of British textiles overseas. Approximately two-thirds of the Studio's work was bought by French manufacturers. Some of its output was marketed through middlemen 31,135 such as Richard Stanway, whose buying and selling of other people's designs must have 146,101 accounted for a large part of his trade as a warehouseman and furnisher.

Not all studios were concerned with the design of fashionable furnishing textiles nor were they all situated in London. A quite different kind of studio was that of Joseph Waterhouse, in Altrincham, outside Manchester, which designed textiles for export to the East. Employing forty designers, most of whom were recruited from Manchester School of Art, it worked almost exclusively for Manchester cotton printers whose main clients were in Turkey, Persia, India, China and Japan. Most of the designers specialized in one aspect of the market.[5]

Most free-lance designers usually worked alone although some took on assistants. Lewis F. Day employed Beatrice Waldram for six years, specializing in embroidery design,[6] while Christopher Dresser's assistants were responsible for most of the later designs attri-

buted to him, including many supplied to the Lancashire printing firm of F. Steiner.[7]

A few decorative artists like Walter Crane produced commercial designs and did not mind whether these were used for wallpapers or fabrics. However, the majority of textile designers drew for specific techniques and, with the full knowledge of the limitations involved, devised workable repeating patterns. Some went even further in the preparation of their work. Point-papers signed by Voysey can be found in the archives of the carpet manufacturers Tomkinson and Adam of Kidderminster. Many of Voysey's designs made 102 for Alexander Morton show a similar professional knowledge, with technical notes and suggestions as to how effects could be achieved.

The free-lance designer of the late nineteenth century had to be both businessman and artist. Day was one of the most commercially aware, adapting his style to suit the tastes of his many clients. Despite his considerable success, he felt the designer's position to be invidious: 'From being himself the maker and seller of his work he has become the servant of the manufacturer who is in turn the servant of the tradesman'.[8] Day did much to encourage a greater understanding between the designer, manufacturer and retailer, though this often meant criticism of his fellow designers. He felt that many were not

100. Arthur Silver.

101. Silver Studio: roller-printed cotton. The design was sold to Richard Stanway in January 1895 for £5.5s. The textile, printed in Mulhouse, was available through Liberty's shops in London and Paris.

102. C. F. A. Voysey: 'Halcyone', watercolour and pencil design, dated June 1898. The pattern was made specially for Alexander Morton & Co.'s 'Rowallan' range. Voysey has noted on his drawing: 'It is hoped that the broken effect of colour in the background can be got by mixing the colour of the bird and sea together *horizontally.'*

professional enough in their attitude or commercial enough in their designs.[9] As a result, in some circles he was seen as a traditionalist out of step with modern workshop practices in which the designer often had the upper hand.

As firms recognized the commercial value of good modern design the free-lance designer benefited. Many patterns required new techniques or the revival of old ones, including discharge and resist printing and stencilling. In turn, manufacturers found ways in which to achieve these effects. Encouraged by such innovations and an atmosphere which sought out technical experimentation, a number of small specialist firms opened. Day in his remarks on the Arts and Crafts Exhibition of 1896 applauded the 'younger generation of workmen who are taking up the ground left vacant by the large mercantile producers, and not only doing work which it would have been a pity to leave undone, but doing it well'.[10] The close association of designers with these small firms proved of paramount importance

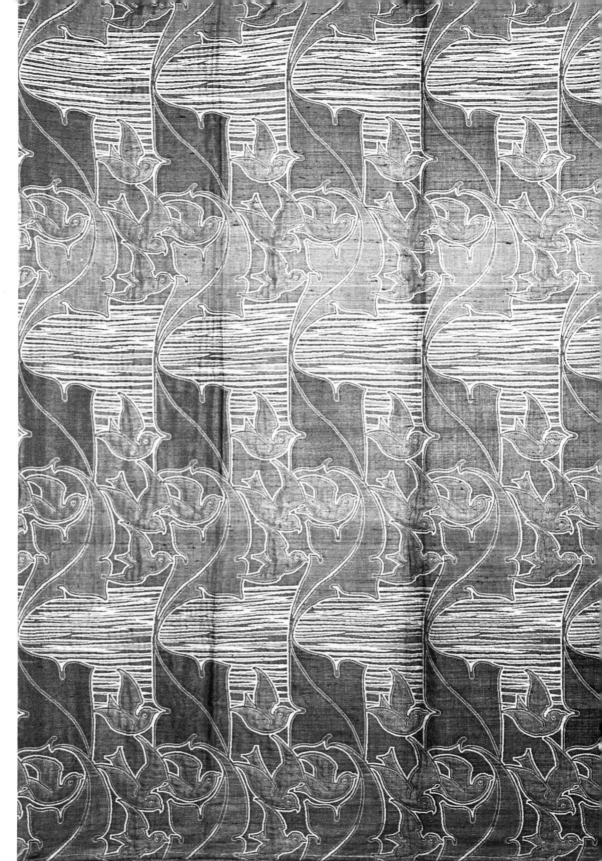

103. C. F. A. Voysey: silk and wool double cloth woven by Alexander Morton & Co. in 1897. The effect in the background is similar to that which Voysey wished to achieve in the 'Halcyone' (Ill. 102).

104. *(opposite)* Lindsay P. Butterfield: 'The Lomond', a 'Liberty Art Fabric' of silk and wool double cloth woven by Alexander Morton & Co. c.1896 and sold for 6s. 6d. a yard.

105. Lewis F. Day: 'The Grotesque', design in watercolour and Chinese white, dated 1886. It was manufactured as a roller-printed cotton by Turnbull and Stockdale and probably shown at the 1888 Exhibition.

not only to their success but also to the organization of the industry in the twentieth
century. Turnbull appointed Day Artistic Director in 1881 and the designs he produced for
the firm in the early years must be considered the main reason for Turnbull and Stockdale's
success. Arthur Lee similarly benefited from the skills of his brother-in-law, G. Faulkner
Armitage, a Manchester designer who had previously provided patterns for Macclesfield
silk weavers.

14,17,
28,62,
105

The improved status of textile designers within the industry and the publicity they
achieved through exhibitions and magazines made many of them as well known as the
leading painters and sculptors of the day. They sold their work not only directly to
manufacturers but also to warehousemen and shops and even, in isolated cases, to commercial studios,[11] and from this economic power came artistic freedom. The business contracts
which Alexander Morton drew up with Voysey and Butterfield specified only that they
would provide a certain number of designs each year which would be exclusive to Morton in
his capacity as a manufacturer of carpets and woven textiles. Both designers subsequently

duplicated many of these patterns and sold them to wallpaper manufacturers and fabric printers, so these 'unique' designs can be found in the archives of two or three different manufacturers.

The organization in 1896 of a Society of Designers, founded 'to support the dignity of the profession, and for friendly social intercourse', was a significant step forward. Butterfield, Haité and J. Scarratt Rigby were all founder members and early officers, and other members included such famous names as Crane, Voysey, George R. Rigby and W. G. Paulson Townsend. Among trade and manufacturing representatives were Lasenby Liberty and Alexander Morton. The group adopted the motto 'Hand, Heart and Head'. Monthly meetings were held for discussions, lectures and the exhibition of members' work. In January 1899 the President, Haité, showed some of his own plant drawings and patterns by his late father, George Haité, the Paisley shawl designer. At the February meeting the Vice-President, Stuart Proverbs, presented over one hundred of his original designs, sketches, photographs, wallpapers, cretonnes, woven silks and wools and stamped and printed velveteens.[12] This openness by designers, who no longer feared the plagiarism of their work, demonstrated their increasing confidence, the result of popular recognition and a greater prosperity in their particular market.

Manufacturers continued to register designs with the Patent Office, some more frequently than others. Both A. H. Lee and G. P. & J. Baker announced their debut by registering their first designs,[13] but after this neither firm did so consistently. Printers such as the Rossendale Printing Company, Daniel Lee, Strines Printing Company and Tootal Broadhurst Lee were regular applicants, but as much of their work in the 1880s and 1890s was for the highly competitive export market, the protection of their designs is understandable. Of the printed textile manufacturers who exhibited with the Arts and Crafts Society, only Morris & Co., Turnbull and Stockdale and Thomas Wardle regularly applied for registration and they tended to protect fabrics showing specific techniques such as indigo discharge and duplex printing or particularly unusual patterns.

Richard Stanway, Lasenby Liberty,[14] Scott Richmond & Co., C. Hindley & Sons and other furnishers and shops also registered work they had bought from free-lance designers. They then commissioned printing or weaving firms to make up the fabrics to be sold in their shops exclusively. In 1904 Liberty acquired the Littler Brothers Print Works at Merton Abbey, but still used contract printers as well. The provenance of many of Liberty's fabrics is extremely complicated. Surviving records show that the Swaisland Print Works produced printed fabrics directly commissioned by the shop (they have their own code in the Works block- and roller-print pattern books), while at the same time G. P. & J. Baker, who owned the Swaisland Works, had their own designs printed there and then sold many of these to Liberty's!

The versatility of manufacturers guaranteed their success. Many undertook contract work for other manufacturers and for shops and by doing so helped to finance their own experimental work. Old techniques were revived, and more modern processes up-dated. Roller-printing was improved and, as has been said, jacquard weaving made more efficient. Synthetic dyestuffs were also improved and put to commercial use. Those who were willing to use good modern designs and adopt sympathetic techniques found little difficulty in selling their work.

In order to attract the custom of both London shops and foreign buyers, manufacturers found it necessary to have a base in London, and most of the leading firms can be found in *Kelly's Directories* at the end of the nineteenth century. Some are listed for the first time, coincidentally, in the late 1880s. The addresses of manufacturers and agents are often identical, suggesting that the latter probably acted on behalf of the manufacturers. William Bennett, a 'Manufacturers Agent and Merchant', shared premises at 231 Oxford Street with A. H. Lee and with Turnbull and Stockdale, and Bennett's stationery was used for a delivery note enclosed with some Turnbull velveteens sent to the 1903 Arts and Crafts Exhibition.[15] Some manufacturers had their own office, but often this can have been hardly more than a desk. In 1897 Edmund Potter was one of thirty-five different firms at 20 Cheapside. The other companies were mostly in allied textile trades (including a silk agent), but they also included a briar pipe maker, a cigarette importer, a wine merchant and a solicitor.

106. Turnbull and Stockdale advertisement from the period 1899-1900, with fashionable typography (compare Debenham and Freebody's advertisement for Wardle, p.152).

DECORATIVE FABRICS
PRINTED TISSUES.
CRETONNES.
VELVETEENS, &c.

For Hangings and Upholstery Purposes. Produced under the Supervision of LEWIS F. DAY.
BY
TURNBULL & STOCKDALE LTD.
· Oxford Circus Avenue ·
231, OXFORD STREET. W.

WORKS · IRWELL · PRINT · WORKS · STACKSTEADS ·
ROSEBANK · PRINT · WORKS · STUBBINS · LANCS

Colour plates

107. Point-paper for a woven textile manufactured by A. H. Lee & Sons in March 1897 – probably from a Harry Napper design – painted in the firm's studio. Each coloured square indicates the lifting of a warp thread on a jacquard loom.

108-111. Four roller-printed cottons manufactured by F. Steiner & Co. This firm bought patterns from most of the leading designers and studios, although few can be identified today. These examples were registered in 1902 (108), 1903 (109, 110) and 1906 (111).

112. Christopher Dresser: roller-printed cotton manufactured by F. Steiner & Co. for Newman, Smith and Newman, c. 1898.

113. Panel of Leek Embroidery worked in wools, silks, gold thread and silver sequins on a cream tusser silk ground which had first been printed with the design by Thomas Wardle. Embroidered by Frances Mary Templeton in 1892.

114. Block-printed cushion cover designed by the Silver Studio and registered by Liberty's in January 1904.

115. Printed or stencilled 'Liberty Art Velveteen' cushion cover. Bought in Zurich in December 1899 from the shop of Robert Furtwängler.

116. 'The Angel with the Tree', embroidered picture worked in silks on a linen ground by Una Taylor to a design by W. Graham Robertson. At the 1903 Exhibition it was for sale at £20.

117. George C. Haité: wool and cotton woven fabric with a printed warp, manufactured by A. H. Lee & Sons in 1903. The V&A owns point-papers for this and the textile in Ill. 118.

118. Wool and cotton fabric woven by A. H. Lee & Sons c. 1899, possibly designed by Harry Napper.

119. Walter Crane: watercolour design for a carpet manufactured as a machine-woven Brussels by Templeton & Co. c. 1895 and shown in the 1903 Exhibition. Crane's working drawing is on squared paper, but it does not function as a point-paper.

120. Lindsay P. Butterfield: 'Hydrangea', watercolour design for a roller-printed cotton manufactured by G. P. & J. Baker for Liberty's, c. 1896. The lower panel giving technical information was added in the Baker studio.

107

108

10

110

11

11

K mart

Hoover Bags
"Encore Supreme"
Semi-gloss
Dutch Boy Paint
2 gals.
_____
o
Masking tape?
_____
o
Deep nap roller
_____

Order Paint
8 gals Navajo
        White
pick up
   30th or 31st

114

115

113

116

117

118

Des." *Hydrangea*"

8 ROLLERS

1 . 2 . 3 . 4 . 5 6 7 8 3/4 4/7

The ground of the Black rollers 36 to the inch
" other rollers 40/45 to the inch

The second Red No 3/4 is like a part etch of No 3 on the full he.
" Yellow No 4/7 is like etched from No 4
These rollers are to be part etch not stipple

120

Many large London shops stocked the new artistic textiles as well as their more traditional furnishings whilst other modernized completely. Several smaller specialist shops opened in the 1880s and 1890s, tending to sell a homogeneous range of home furnishings. At least one, Wardle & Co. in Bond Street (run from 1883 to 1888 by Thomas Wardle and W. S. Brough), sold only fabrics. In the mid-1890s three Regent Street shops –
121 Liberty's, A. Stephens & Co. and F. B. Goodyer's Aesthetic Gallery – specialized in 'Art
122 Fabrics' and it is difficult to understand how the market coped with such competition. Furnishing trade magazines do list a great number of shops going into liquidation at the end of the century. Most fashionable customers preferred small specialist shops, so it is not surprising to see large organizations foundering. The *Furniture Gazette* for 15 May 1896 lists one firm, Frank Giles & Company of Kensington High Street, as having eighty-seven creditors when it was forced to close, among them Morris & Co., the upholsterers (later printers) Newman, Smith and Newman, the carpet manufacturers Brinton's, James Templeton & Co. and Woodward Grosvenor & Co., and the textile companies of Alexander Morton, H. C. McCrea and G. P. & J. Baker. The influence of Ambrose Heal on his family's business at the end of the nineteenth century was dramatic, and what had been a specialist bed and mattress maker became one of the most fashionable shops in London.
123 They bought fabrics from all the leading producers of the day, including G. P. & J. Baker, Thomas Wardle, Newman, Smith and Newman, Alexander Morton, Donald Brothers, A. H. Lee and Turnbull and Stockdale, and from the agents Bennett and Stanway.[16] Liberty's also reorganized, and although they continued to be one of the largest importers of Eastern goods their shop looked less like an exotic bazaar. The attractive floral textiles which they commissioned and sold at this time established their own very special British style.

The commercial development of embroidery workshops during the latter part of the nineteenth century was much simpler than that of textile production. Several organizations followed the example of the Royal School of Art Needlework, employing embroideresses not only to work new designs and special commissions but also to repair and clean embroideries and tapestries – the forerunners of modern textile conservation workshops. The standard of professional work improved with experience and, besides its reputation for artistic designs in silk and crewel wools, the Royal School of Art Needlework became renowned for gold and silver thread embroidery for official and ceremonial wear. Previously this had been produced in small specialist workshops. This combination of traditional and experimental skills is the school's most enduring quality.

145   In its formative years the Royal School of Art Needlework commissioned designs from
124 leading artists and designers such as Walter Crane, Edward Burne-Jones, W. G. Paulson
132 Townsend and Selwyn Image. From the 1890s many embroidery schools employed their own designers, of whom Nellie Wichelo of the Royal School and Mary Gemmell of the Decorative Needlework Society are perhaps the best known. Both took part in the Arts and Crafts Exhibitions. The significant rise in the number of women designers was encouraged by the amount of work being exhibited by women at this time. Improved opportunities in art education and a more liberal attitude within middle-class families had helped to make the profession of designer acceptable. *The Studio*'s view was surprisingly old-fashioned: it felt that an improvement in women's designs for embroidery had developed from their

domestic duties, 'the planning of carpets and curtains giving the embroiderer a greater breadth of treatment and a keener sense of proportion and decorative line'.[17] The Society of Women Artists and the Women's Guild of Art were established to benefit women designers and to provide opportunities for the public display of urban and rural crafts. Most of the celebrated rural workshops founded to revive traditional embroidery and lace were dependent on women, both as workers and as designers. They sold their crafts throughout Britain and at the Rural Industries Co-operative Society in New Bond Street, London. What had started out as a means of providing a livelihood in deprived areas thus supplied sought-after furnishings for fashionable society.

Embroidery patterns were also commissioned by magazines. *Arts and Crafts* and many of the more traditional ladies' journals published line drawings by well known designers.[18] *Home Art-Work* went even further and entered finished versions of some of their printed patterns in the Arts and Crafts Exhibitions: four panels shown in 1890 had been worked from the designs of M. Bowley,[19] Kate Clarke and George C. Haité by the Decorative Needlework Society and other notable embroideresses such as Mrs Conyers Morrell.

Thomas Wardle printed silks, cottons and velveteens especially for embroidery.
113 Initially these were intended for the Leek Embroidery Society, established by his wife, but soon he was providing them for Liberty's to sell in their shops.[20] Artistically designed,

121. Music room designed and furnished by Goodyer's, 1905. Appliqué hangings are used here with a matching Donegal carpet of tree motifs.

SEVEN·HOVRS·TO·WORK·TO·SOOTHING·SLVMBER·SEVEN,
TEN·TO·THE·WORLD·ALLOT·AND·ALL·TO·HEAVEN"

122. Bedroom designed by Liberty's and displayed in their Regent Street shop in 1897.

123. Heal's 'hygienic' bed with 'Tiger Lily' bedcover, designed by Lindsay P. Butterfield in 1896 (see Ill. 8) and printed for the shop by G. P. & J. Baker.

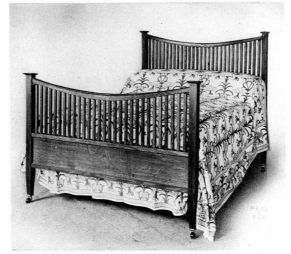

ready-printed kits (complete with embroidery silks and needles) took over in popularity from Berlin woolwork. They were available from established drapers, such as Pearsalls and Maison Helbronner, and also from fashionable shops such as Morris & Co. and Liberty's.[21]

The frequent buying trips to Britain by foreign traders coupled with the work of British agents abroad led to a flood of British textiles in Europe and America. British textiles proved particularly popular when displayed in the Philadelphia Centennial Exposition of 1876, and were sold through such leading shops as Woodville & Co. in Philadelphia, Cowtan & Tout of Madison Avenue in New York, and Marshall Field in Chicago. Liberty's excellent business organization was a vital factor in developing their international reputation. Their Paris shop, which they opened in 1890 at 38 avenue de l'Opéra, became a popular centre not only for the French but for most of fashionable Europe. Continental museums bought textiles there and the shop became so famous that in Italy Art Nouveau design is known as 'Stile Liberty'. Although there are strong stylistic differences between designs of the British Arts and Crafts Movement and Continental Art Nouveau, the influence of British work, and particularly of the textiles available in Europe, can be clearly seen. Like the Arts and Crafts Movement itself, the international success of British fabrics in the late nineteenth and early twentieth century is attributable to two equally important factors: well drawn imaginative designs and innovative production. Highly organized successful retailing helped to bring British textiles to the attention of the more discerning public throughout the Western world.

124. Selwyn Image: 'Atlanta', design for embroidery, c. 1890. Image drew many similar repeating designs for the Royal School of Art Needlework.

125. Harry Napper: 'Teazle', watercolour design for a printed cotton manufactured by G. P. & J. Baker in 1899.

This section lists the most important individuals and establishments concerned with British textile production in the late nineteenth and early twentieth centuries. Most took part in the Arts and Crafts Exhibitions; non-exhibitors are included if their work was significant. Unless otherwise stated, exhibition details refer to the London Arts and Crafts Exhibitions, and other locations are in London. Where relevant there is an indication of the holdings of the Victoria and Albert Museum (V&A), which before the turn of the century was called the South Kensington Museum. References to other individuals, groups and firms will be found through the Index. A dagger (†) in the margin indicates that full picture references will be found in the Index.

Aller Vale Industries Rural industry set up in Newton Abbot, Devon, and known chiefly for pottery. They exhibited pillow lace, ramie lace and 'village needlework' in 1889.

Angus, Christine Drummond (1877–1921) Designer and embroideress. The second wife of Walter Sickert, she produced designs for various media including stencilling, furniture and embroidery. Her textiles often use figurative designs with children. The V&A owns a cot cover embroidered in 1908 and Westminster Abbey a dalmatic made for a children's service.

Armitage, G. Faulkner (1849–1937) Architect and designer of metalwork, furniture, wallpaper and textiles. He lived and worked at Stamford in Altrincham in Cheshire, and designed repeating patterns for woven textiles manufactured by J. O. Nicholson of Macclesfield and by A. H. Lee, his brother-in-law. He also produced designs for the Macclesfield School of Embroidery and the Royal School of Art Needlework. He taught art at Macclesfield School of Art and showed three furnished rooms at the 1895 Manchester Arts and Crafts Exhibition.

Ashbee, Charles Robert (1863–1942) Architect and founder of the Guild of Handicrafts started in London in 1888 which moved to Chipping Camden in 1902. Best known as a designer of metalwork and jewellery, in 1889 he exhibited an embroidered piano cover worked by his mother, Mrs H. S. Ashbee (V&A).

Baker, G. P. & J. Printed fabric manufacturers, founded by † two sons of George Baker, a gardener turned trader, working in Istanbul in the second half of the nineteenth century. George Percival Baker, the eldest son, was sent to London in the 1880s to run the English end of the company and was soon trading on his own account. In 1893 he took his brother, James, into partnership and with the acquisition of the Swaisland Print Works in Crayford they soon became manufacturers. Their first products included printed wools, silks and stencilled linen table covers. Although G. P. Baker remained the controlling force of the firm until his death in 1951, many of the early designs used were selected by Charles Percival, his cousin, who bought work from all the leading designers, among them Voysey, Butterfield, Haité, Mawson and the Silver Studio. Textiles produced in the first ten years were characterized by highly original floral patterns. Since then the firm has specialized in the adaptation of historic designs. G. P. & J. Baker printed textiles under their own name and, as owners of the Swaisland Works, became contract printers to many leading shops of the day including Liberty's, Heal's and Story's. Printed silks, cottons and linens by Cecil Millar, Allan Vigers and Joseph Doran were exhibited between 1903 and 1916. The V&A has a good collection of printed fabrics and original designs given by the firm in the 1960s and these formed part of the Museum's exhibition *From East to West* (1984).

Barlow, Hannah (active 1870–1913) Ceramicist and sculptor. She exhibited a child's woven bedspread and an embroidered table-cloth and cushion cover in 1912.

Batten, John Dicksen (1860–1932) Painter and illustrator. He is known to have designed three exhibited textiles: 'Psyche before Persephone', embroidered by Agnes Day (shown in 1896), a second needlework panel, worked by Una Taylor (1899), and a tapestry woven for Hindhead Chapel by William Sleath (1912). The tapestry was later displayed in the War Memorials Exhibition at the V&A in 1920.

Birmingham School of Art One of the most progressive art schools of the late nineteenth century; in 1896 it headed the National Competition awards for the fifth year running. Under the first two headmasters, E. R. Taylor and Robert

98

Catterson Smith, it gained a reputation for high standards of draughtsmanship and originality of design. Teaching concentrated on the applied arts, especially decorative painting, metalwork (including jewellery and enamelling) and embroidery. Mary Newill taught there, with May Morris acting as visiting lecturer. Several panels were embroidered by the students from their designs. Many ex-students and teachers became famous as free-lance artists and designers or members of the Bromsgrove Guild of Applied Arts. A number produced designs for embroidery, including Henry Payne, C. M. Gere, Joseph Southall, Offlow Scattergood and Bernard Sleigh. Between 1893 and 1916 the school exhibited embroideries and designs for lace and printed fabrics.

Blount, Godfrey (1859–1937) Designer, trained at the Slade School. In 1896 he founded the Peasant Art Society, part of the Haslemere Peasant Industries, with his wife, Ethel Hine, and sister-in-law, Mrs Maud Egerton King. Blount was 43, responsible for designing all appliqué embroideries (called 58,59 'Peasant Tapestries') and hand-woven pile and tapestry carpets made at Haslemere. He exhibited work in 1896 and 1899 and was also involved in the Home Arts and Industries Association (he was a Committee member) and the Clarion Guild. The V&A owns two hangings and a set of valances.

Bromsgrove Guild of Applied Arts An association for craftsmen set up *c.* 1897 chiefly by ex-students and teachers of Birmingham School of Art. The Guild, through its members, had workshops in Rugby (specializing in printing), Birmingham (furniture, stained glass, mosaic, wood-engraving, decorative painting, jewellery and embroidery) and Bromsgrove (plaster and metalwork). Each section was financed and controlled separately by one of the guildsmen, who were also responsible for training apprentices. Mary Newill ran the embroidery section and several projects were completed under her direction, including the *Faerie Queene* 73 panels (1897). These were exhibited in 1899 and shown again as part of a room by the Guild in the British Pavilion at the Paris Exhibition of 1900.

Buckle, Mary (active 1888–1906) Embroideress, known chiefly for needlework designed by Lewis F. Day. The two collaborated on *Art in Needlework* (1901), for which she was technical adviser. The illustrations – some of which were exhibited in 1899 – show her skills in fine silk embroidery. Between 1888 and 1906 she exhibited twenty embroideries worked by herself and by others. All but two were from Day's designs.

Burden, Bessie (Elizabeth) (1842–1924) Embroideress. The sister of Jane (Mrs William) Morris, she learned her skills in the Morris home and for a time was employed professionally by Morris & Co. She taught at the Royal School of Art Needlework in the 1870s and was responsible for supervising its exhibits at the 1876 Centennial Exposition in Philadelphia. A form of crewelwork she had perfected in early Morris embroideries was used for the figurative Walter Crane hangings displayed there. She became an examiner for the Board of Education. Her exhibits, in 1888 and 1890, included three panels depicting classical female figures originally embroidered in 1861 for the Morrises' first home, the Red House. The scheme was not finished and the panels were made up into a screen and sold after the exhibition to George Howard, Earl of Carlisle.

Burne-Jones, Edward (1834–98) Artist and close friend of William Morris. He supplied figurative designs for tapestries woven by Morris & Co. and with Morris designed a number of embroideries for Morris & Co., the Royal School of Art Needlework, and family and friends. Tapestries exhibited were 'St Cecilia' (1888), 'Peace' (1889), 'Flora' (1890), part of the Holy Grail series (1893), and 'Angeli Laudantes' and 'Angeli Ministrantes' (1896). 'Love', a panel embroidered by Frances Horner, was shown in 1896, and sketches for 'The Passing of Venus' in 1899 and 1916. The V&A owns one tapestry, 'Angeli Laudantes', and a set of early embroideries based on the Arthurian legend worked by his wife, Georgiana.

Burtchall, Mrs Somerset Organizer of a school in Rome utilizing the skills of local embroideresses, especially Jewish women. The patterns, mostly worked in linen, were based on historic Italian designs. Embroideries exhibited in 1889 and 1890 included four 'Roman Aprons'.

Butterfield, Lindsay P. (1869–1948) One of the most im- † portant and successful designers of the period, he produced repeating patterns for wallpapers and woven and printed textiles. He left school at eighteen and worked in a West India merchant's office 1887–8, while attending night classes at Lambeth School of Art. After a short stay in the architectural office of his cousin, Philip Johnstone, he spent three years at the National Art Training School at South Kensington and won a number of awards while still a student, including an Owen Jones prize in the National Competition of 1890. His first commission, in 1892, was for a wallpaper, and within two years he had established himself as a free-lance designer. He taught at a number of art

126. Caricature of Lindsay P. **Butterfield** by Robert Percy Gossop, drawn on an envelope addressed to Mrs Butterfield, 1901.

schools, notably Kingston-upon-Thames and the Central School of Arts and Crafts, and was a founder member of the Society of Designers. In 1922 he published *Floral Forms in Historic Design* with his friend W. G. Paulson Townsend. Butterfield sold patterns to most of Britain's leading manufacturers: the V&A owns examples of his work for G. P. & J. Baker, Warner & Sons, Thomas Wardle, Turnbull and Stockdale and Alexander Morton, with whom he signed a contract in 1902. He also supplied designs to Newman, Smith and Newman and David Barbour. Only four of his patterns were exhibited: a design for cretonne in 1893, a sample of 'Lilium' fabric shown by Alexander Morton in 1896, and two designs for woven fabrics in 1903.

Button, Kate Designer and embroideress, known only for a few pictorial embroideries including 'Winter', exhibited in 1906, and 'Where Seagulls Play', shown in 1910. These were highly praised in the press.

Canterbury Weavers Established in 1897 in premises in King's Bridge, Canterbury, previously used by Flemish and Huguenot weavers. By 1902 the firm employed thirty local women. Hand-woven rugs and fabrics were made, including linens and wools, 'Canterbury Silks' and 'Canterbury Muslins'. They showed work at the Home Arts and Industries Exhibition, where in 1902 they won the highest prize for a rug.

Carpenter, Alfred (active 1895–1912) Decorative painter and designer of printed and woven textiles who adopted a traditional style for his patterns, including reproductions of historic designs. He trained at Birkbeck School of Art (part of the South Kensington Schools) and in 1895 gained a silver medal in the National Competition. He sold designs to Howarth & Co., David Barbour, Turnbull and Stockdale and Gardner and Bayley of Manchester. Between 1896 and 1912 he exhibited twelve designs and five textiles; and in 94 1899 and 1900 he also showed textile designs at the Royal Academy. The V&A owns one printed cotton designed by him.

Cave, Walter (1863–1939) Architect and designer. Lace and embroidery to his designs were exhibited, including a Honiton lace superfrontal made by local women for Sidbury Church, Devon, and a matching embroidered frontal, both shown in 1899. His wife and daughter were also regular exhibitors (in 1890, 1899 and 1903) with embroideries and lace after designs by him and by May and William Morris.

Central School of Arts and Crafts Started in 1896 by the Technical Education Board of London County Council under the directorship of George Frampton and W. R. Lethaby; originally at 316 Regent Street, later in purpose-built premises in Holborn. The school charged low fees and concentrated on the technical and artistic training of professionals rather than amateurs. Staff included many of England's leading active designers and artists, notably Maggie Briggs and May Morris for embroidery, Walter Taylor and Luther Hooper for weaving, and L. P. Butterfield, who taught design for some years.

Century Guild Established in 1882 by Arthur Heygate † Mackmurdo and Selwyn Image with Herbert Horne, Benjamin Creswick (sculptor), Clement Heaton (metalworker) and Heywood Sumner. The Guild designed decorative arts of various types which were then produced for it by outside firms such as Simpson & Godlee (printed cottons), A. H. Lee (woven fabrics), and Morris & Co. (early experimental carpets). Similarity in technique suggests that some embroideries were worked by the Leek Embroidery Society. Much of the work was commissioned and sold through the Bond Street shop of Wilkinson & Sons. The Guild displayed textiles, upholstered furniture and a carpet at the Health Exhibition of 1884, the Liverpool International Exhibition of 1886 and the Inventions Exhibition in 1887. The Arts and Crafts Exhibition of 1888 included a rug and embroidered screen designed by Mackmurdo and hangings by Horne. The V&A owns five printed cottons, an embroidered cloth, three woven fabrics and a carpet fragment.

Christie, Grace (Mrs A. G. I.) (1872–1938) Designer, weaver and 'perhaps the most skilled embroideress of her generation' (W. G. Paulson Townsend). She trained at the Slade School. Her publications include *Embroidery and Tapestry Weaving* (1906), *Samplers and Stitches* (1920) and *English Medieval Embroidery* (1938), and she edited the magazine *Needle and Thread* from 1914. An energetic and inspiring teacher, in 1909 she was appointed as the first embroidery lecturer at the Royal College of Art where she remained until 1921. Her work is revivalist in style and technique. She exhibited embroideries and tapestries between 1903 and 1916. These included many technical diagrams and samplers, some taken from historic examples. In 1916 she, her husband Archibald Christie and F. W. Troup (architect of the Art Workers' Guild) exhibited a bedroom for a small country house with white embroidered hangings. The V&A owns several of her linen and cotton samplers and one panel worked in coloured silks.

Clare Embroidery Blue or red monochrome cotton embroidery worked in trailing floral designs on linen and silk. The first class was set up in 1895 by Mrs Florence Vere O'Brien in Newhall, Ennis, Co. Clare, in Ireland to help to train poor local women. She was assisted by Mina Keppie, a Scottish embroideress who became manageress of the various classes producing a range of articles for the fashionable market. The Ballyana class specialized in children's clothing worked on Liberty 'art' silks. Mrs Vere O'Brien was also involved in reviving Limerick lace and founding a lace school. Both embroidery and lace were exhibited nationally and internationally.

Clarion Guild of Handicrafts Started in 1902 in Manchester by Mrs Julia Dawson of the *Clarion*, the leading English Socialist newspaper. The Guild was originally organized for local craftsmen and at first members worked together in the evenings. Crafts included furniture, pottery, metalwork, embroidery, stained glass, bookbinding, illuminated books, posters and stencilling. By 1904 there were branches all over Britain, with a London headquarters at 48 George Street, Hampstead Road. Annual exhibitions were held in which leading designers and craftsmen showed their work alongside amateurs. Ann Macbeth, Godfrey Blount and Heal's were all exhibitors.

Crane, Walter (1845–1915) Founder member and first President of the Arts and Crafts Exhibition Society. One of the best known and most versatile artists and designers of his generation: painter in oils, watercolour, tempera and gesso, calligrapher, book illustrator and designer of wallpaper, stained glass, metalwork, tiles and pottery, embroideries, tapestries, carpets and woven and printed fabrics. He served an apprenticeship as a wood engraver 1859–62 and then worked as a book illustrator, designer and painter. His first submission to the Royal Academy was accepted in 1862. He was also an art theorist and educationalist, Principal of the Royal College of Art 1898–9, and an examiner at the National Art Training School at South Kensington. He lectured and published extensively on the theory of design, his most influential works being *The Bases of Design* (1898) and *Line and Form* (1900). His numerous articles include 'Needlework as a Mode of Artistic Expression' (*Magazine of Art*, 1897–8). He was very well known abroad, travelled frequently and was associated with many foreign as well as British artistic groups. Between 1888 and 1912 he exhibited designs for carpets, printed cottons and damasks as well as finished carpets (Templeton's), printed silks, cottons and velveteens (Thomas Wardle and Birch, Gibson & Co.), damasks (Ireland Brothers, John Wilson) and embroideries worked by his wife and daughter, Una Taylor, Mrs Conyers Morrell and others. The V&A owns a number of his textile designs (including some for dress and one tapestry cartoon), as well as printed and woven textiles, damasks, embroideries and carpet samples.

Davis, Louis (1861–1941) Designer and book illustrator. He designed two embroideries exhibited in 1890 and 1893, both worked by Nora Harris. In the 1908 Summer Exhibition at the New Gallery he showed a banner of St George and the Dragon embroidered by his wife which was presented to the Governor-General of Canada.

Day, Lewis F. (1845–1910) Founder member of the Arts and Crafts Exhibition Society and one of the most commercially aware and successful designers of his generation. He studied in Brighton, in France, and for two years in Germany. He worked as a stained glass artist 1865–70 and taught

127. Portrait of Lewis F. **Day** as Master of the Art Workers' Guild by Edward R. Hughes, 1897.

128. J. H. **Dearle**: 'Ispahan', woollen fabric woven by Morris & Co., c. 1888. Shown at the 1896 Exhibition as a William Morris design.

on a part-time basis. From 1870 he produced free-lance designs for textiles of all kinds, wallpaper, ceramics, silver and furniture. He wrote numerous articles and reviews for the *British Architect* (his first published in 1878), *Art Journal, Magazine of Art* and *Manchester Guardian*. He published many books on the theory of pattern-making, among them *Instances of Accessory Art* (1880), *The Planning of Ornament* (1887) and *Ornament and its Application* (1904). His publications concerning textiles include biographical articles on William Morris and other contemporary designers and the embroidery manual *Art in Needlework*, written with Mary Buckle (1901). He taught and lectured on design and was an Examiner in Painting and Ornament for the Board of Education. In 1881 he became the Artistic Director of Turnbull and Stockdale, giving 'a unity to the firm's goods'. His style is often derivative and eclectic but his draughtsmanship excellent. He sold designs to many textile manufacturers and shops, notably John Wilson and William Fry (table damasks), Brinton's (carpets), Alexander Morton (Madras muslins), A. H. Lee (woven textiles), Royal Windsor Tapestry Company (tapestry), and Thomas Wardle and Turnbull and Stockdale (printed textiles). Between 1888 and 1910 he exhibited designs and fans, lace, woven and printed textiles and many embroideries, the latter worked by Mary Buckle and his wife, Ruth Emma Day. He also submitted fabrics to other leading shows including the Manchester Arts and Crafts Exhibitions, and in 1881 and 1884 four of his textile designs were shown at the Royal Academy. The V&A owns a large collection of his designs and textiles, including printed cottons, linens and velveteens by Thomas Wardle and Turnbull and Stockdale (who presented a number in 1954), two embroideries (a fire-screen and a bodice front) and a lace collar and cuffs.

Dearle, John Henry (1860–1932) Designer and craftsman. †
He first began work at Morris & Co. in 1878 as assistant in the Oxford Street shop. His artistic talents were soon noticed by Morris who trained him as a tapestry weaver. He produced his first tapestry design in 1887 and by 1890 was the firm's chief textile designer. His early textiles are closely based on Morris's style but his mature work, which is influenced by Near Eastern patterns, shows greater originality. He designed tapestries, carpets, embroideries and woven and printed fabrics and supervised most textile production up to and after Morris's death in 1896, and later became Art Director. He continued to run the Merton Abbey Works until his own death in 1932. Because of Morris's popularity, Dearle's contribution has been sadly neglected and many of his exhibited designs (especially those in the 1899 Morris

retrospective) were described as Morris's. In later exhibitions his work was correctly attributed. The V&A owns designs, examples of most of his best printed and woven textiles, plus embroideries and one Wilton carpet.

Decorative Needlework Society An offshoot of the Royal School of Art Needlework, founded *c.* 1879 'with the laudable object of reviving high-class embroidery, and thereby affording employment to many ladies whose skilled fingers could not find due reward without efficient organisation' (*Art Workers' Quarterly*, III, 1904). It taught embroidery and produced all kinds of artistic and traditional needlework including restoration. From the early twentieth century weaving and the repair of tapestries were undertaken. Mary Gemmell, who provided most of the Society's designs, became manageress in 1895. The society was present at every exhibition and displayed embroidered *portières*, curtains, quilts, altar frontals, panels and other items. In 1906 it exhibited a working tapestry loom. It was also credited with the preparation and mounting of other exhibitors' work.

Donegal Industrial Fund Set up in Ireland in 1883 by Mrs Ernest Hart to help bring prosperity to areas stricken by the famine of 1880. She encouraged the revival of local crafts – lace-making, tweed and linen weaving, hand spinning, dyeing and embroidery. Classes were taught by local gentry who had themselves been badly affected. A style of embroidery called 'Kells' was developed, worked in a polished flax thread on linen and wool with patterns taken from illuminated Celtic manuscripts. In 1887 the Government offered £1,000 to assist the industry and a shop was set up at 31 New Cavendish Street, London. Mrs Hart frequently exhibited Irish handicrafts, including hand-made linens (1896), hand-dyed wools (1888 and 1916), various examples of embroidered linen from Donegal, and Limerick lace designed by the nuns of Kenmare (1888).

Doran, Joseph (active *c.* 1900–1912) Designer of wallpaper, printed and woven textiles, metalwork and enamels. He studied at Belfast School of Art from *c.* 1897, then moved to London and set up his studio in Hounslow. From here he produced textile designs for Alexander Morton, Turnbull 41 and Stockdale, G. P. & J. Baker, Thomas Wardle, and Story's. Between 1906 and 1912 he exhibited printed cottons and linens, panels of embroidery for costume and a lace fan. The V&A owns designs and one small sample of a printed cotton.

Dresser, Christopher (1834–1904) Botanist, design theorist, and one of the most influential artistic figures of the nineteenth century. A leading Aesthetic designer, he is now best known for that early work which shows a strong Japanese influence. He trained for two years from the age of thirteen at Somerset House School of Design. He produced patterns for textiles, metalwork, woodwork, ceramics and 112 wallpaper. In 1862 he published *The Art of Decorative Design*, which was followed by many other books, articles and lectures on botany, design and Japanese art. In 1882 he established a studio at Wellesley Lodge, Sutton, and in 1889 moved this to Elm Bank, Barnes. He sold textile designs to Crossley & Sons, J. W. & C. Ward, Barlow and Jones, F. Steiner, Turnbull and Stockdale, Thomas Wardle, Warner & Sons and John Wilson. He is also known to have acted as art advisor to manufacturers and shops, including the Art Furnishers' Alliance Ltd. Textiles attributed to Dresser from the 1880s show the influence of his highly original, often eccentric earlier patterns, but are likely to be studio work. The V&A owns various attributed designs and textiles.

Dun Emer Industries Founded in 1902 in Dundrum, Co. Dublin, by Evelyn Gleeson with the aim that Irish craftswomen should utilize Irish materials for original crafts. The organization produced printed books, coloured woodcuts and painted fans under the direction of Elizabeth Corbet Yeats. Sections making rugs, tapestries and embroideries were managed by her sister Lily (Susan Mary) Yeats and some designs were supplied by their sister-in-law, Mrs Jack Yeats, wife of the painter. Lily Yeats was a friend of May Morris and was employed 1886–94 as an embroideress by Morris & Co. in London. Many of the designs used by Dun Emer were of Irish origin and these were used for domestic items as well as dress ornament. One lady's costume is now in the National Museum of Ireland. The group took part in a number of Irish crafts shows and the Home Arts and Industries Exhibitions in London.

English Silk Weaving Company Weaving firm in Ipswich with premises in London 1899–1904 at 231 Oxford Street. In 1896 they set up an exhibition with the Spitalfields Silk Association 'to show excellence in quality of pure unweighted silk of home manufacture as grounds for all kinds of embroidery'. Lewis F. Day judged the three classes and prizes were awarded. Three silks were exhibited in 1899 and 1903, including one designed by Archibald Christie. Reginald Warner, listed as a designer and weaver with the firm, was later associated with the Gainsborough Silk Weaving Company.

Fisher, Alexander (1864–1936) Silversmith and enameller, who also designed embroideries. A panel called 'Penelope', worked in outline stitches in silk on linen by his wife and daughter, was exhibited in 1890. Two curtains from a set designed by him and worked by the Royal School of Art Needlework for Fanhams Hall, Ware, are now in the V&A.

Fletcher, Herbert (active 1880s–90s) Textile designer. Six of his designs were exhibited in 1889 and 1890. These included silk damasks, a silk and wool brocatelle woven by H. C. McCrea & Co., a chenille curtain woven by Alexander Morton and Madras muslins exhibited by Lang & Co.

France, Georgie Evelyn Cave (1864–1934) Decorative painter, book illustrator, jewellery designer and embroideress. In 1890 she exhibited two panels of embroidery and a design for a fan. An ex-student of Birmingham School of Art, in 1894 she married Arthur Gaskin (then teaching at the school) and the two became important figures in local artistic circles. She is known to have produced work for the Bromsgrove Guild of Applied Arts but no embroideries can be traced from this association. She is now best known for the jewellery she and her husband designed together.

Gainsborough Silk Weaving Company Manufacturers of hand-woven silks and velvets who exhibited in 1916. Examples of their work were illustrated in the *Studio Year Book* for 1914. All known silks were woven from designs by Reginald Warner.

Garnett, Annie (1864–1942) and **the Spinnery, Windermere** About 1890 Annie Garnett set up a class in Windermere to teach the crafts of hand spinning and weaving which became one of the most successful ventures of the Home Arts and Industries Bureau. The training of local people resulted in a self-supporting commercial enterprise, the Spinnery, 129 producing high quality woollen, silk and linen fabrics, spun and woven by outworkers under Annie Garnett's direction. These became highly sought after by embroiderers and from the late nineteenth century the Spinnery also produced embroideries worked onto these grounds. Concentrating on domestic items, Annie Garnett provided all the designs for woven and embroidered textiles, from traditional patterns for use with traditional techniques to highly original floral motifs worked in a more modern style. Although her embroidery designs are best known today it was hand weaving that interested her most. She published *Handspinning* (1896) and spent much of her time experimenting with the technique, reviving historic structures and using unusual yarns, including metal. Woven textiles were shown in 1903, 1906 and 1912; all were designed by Annie Garnett and often listed under her name. However, all Spinnery weavers involved in this work were identified. No embroideries were ever displayed in Arts and Crafts Exhibitions. Elsewhere throughout Britain the Spinnery showed a great many woven and embroidered textiles, for instance at the Home Arts and Industries and Manchester Arts and Crafts Exhibitions. The V&A owns three examples of her woven textiles: a silk damask stole, a panel of woven silk and a silk and silver 96 tissue.

Gere, Charles M. (1869–1957) Decorative painter and book illustrator who studied and taught at Birmingham School of Art. He designed both church and secular embroideries, four of which were exhibited in 1899, 1903 and 1904. His most celebrated example, a banner made for Worcester Cathedral, was exhibited in 1899, and another notable piece, an altar frontal made for the chapel of Madresfield Court (designed and decorated by members of the Bromsgrove Guild), was shown in 1903.

Gimson, Ernest (1864–1919) Architect and designer. He set up a workshop with Sidney and Ernest Barnsley in Gloucestershire in 1894 and is now best known for his furniture. Embroideries designed by him were exhibited in 1890, 1893, 1896, 1899, 1903 and 1910. Like his furniture, these appear to have been simply worked domestic items.

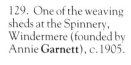

129. One of the weaving sheds at the Spinnery, Windermere (founded by Annie **Garnett**), c.1905.

Glasgow School of Art British decorative design in the twentieth century was highly influenced by the work of students, ex-students and staff at Glasgow School of Art at the end of the nineteenth century. The school's work is best known through four ex-students, Charles Rennie Mackintosh, Herbert McNair and Margaret and Frances Macdonald, but, apart from a few stencilled canvases and individual embroidered panels made as part of interior schemes, they produced few textiles. Mackintosh, George Walton and Jessie M. King all designed textiles later in their careers but it is the school's early production of embroidery which is now legendary. In 1894 a class open to students and outsiders was started by Jessie Newbery, an ex-student and wife of the influential Principal of the school, Francis Newbery. Her individual use of coarse fabrics, pastel colours and plain stitching greatly influenced modern embroidery and, through her Saturday classes for teachers, the development of the craft in schools. What had started as a minor part of the school's curriculum became important and all female students were expected to take embroidery lessons as part of their timetable. The very high standards of design and technique achieved by these classes is only now being full recognized. Mrs Newbery's ideas were continued in the work of one of her pupils, Ann Macbeth, who began teaching at the school in 1901 and who took over the class on her retirement in 1908. The school exhibited embroideries only once, in 1896. By the turn of the century the Glasgow School of

Embroidery (as it became known) was famous and, through the Glasgow Exhibition of 1901 and the Turin Exhibition of 1902, sought after throughout Europe. The V&A owns five embroideries (including two collars and a belt) by Jessie Newbery; an embroidered picture, a tablecloth and a curtain by Ann Macbeth; and a lampshade panel embroidered by Margaret Macdonald for the Hill House, Helensburgh.

Goodyer, Frank Brunton Retailer. He worked for a number of years at Liberty's shop in Regent Street and was in partnership 1887–9 with Arthur Lasenby Liberty. In 1890 he opened his first shop, the Aesthetic Gallery, at 155 New Bond Street, selling 'artistic fabrics and eastern curios'. By 1901 he had premises also at 326 Oxford Street, 174 and 198 Regent Street, and at 114 Brompton Road. Within a year of opening, the Aesthetic Gallery was described as 'a central depot for the distribution of textile fabrics of home manufacture', selling specially printed silks and velvets from Thomas Wardle and others. The firm displayed shadow silks and woven tusser fabrics at the 1895 Manchester Arts and Crafts Exhibition. By the mid 1890s Goodyer's shops extended their range to cover all forms of interior decoration. Rooms decorated by the firm were illustrated in contemporary magazines. From 1904 Goodyer is also listed as a supplier of 'artistic costumes' at 174 Regent Street, one of the two shops still owned by him at that time. Goodyers Ltd continued to trade in London until 1973.

Grasett, Katie (active 1898–1916) Weaver and designer who founded the London School of Weaving in 1898. Its early work concentrated on the production of tapestries but under her direction the school developed a style using traditional hand-loom weaving with new designs and fibres, including aluminium. She exhibited textiles in 1910, 1912 and 1916, including two tapestry pictures and hand-woven silk and gold brocades, gold and aluminium brocades, cloth of gold, and shot silks. These were woven by her and two other members of the school, K. Mannering and M. Thomas. The V&A owns one example of Katie Grasett's work, 'Chariot Wheel', a silk and gold tissue woven in 1910.

Gwatkin, Arthur (active 1887–1900) Designer of wallpapers and fabrics. He had no artistic training but as partner in a firm of decorators realized the difficulties in obtaining good wallpaper designs and started to draw patterns himself. These show a highly original style based on nature which adapted well to stencil decoration and wallpaper friezes for which he is best known. He provided designs for the first examples of stencilled canvas produced by Green and Abbot of Oxford Street. Several of his designs were illustrated in *Der Moderne Stil* in 1895–8.

130 **Haité, George C.** (1855–1924) Designer of fabrics, carpets, wallpapers, woodcarving and reliefs, metalwork, leaded glass and book illustration – although his first love was oil and watercolour painting. A highly original artist, he learned a great deal about the industry from his father, George Haité, a well known Paisley textile designer. He came to London in 1873 and studied at Croydon School of Art. From 1883 he exhibited at the Royal Academy. In 1898 *The Studio* described him as 'an artist whose range is unusually wide and energy extraordinary', listing twenty-two watercolours and oils that he had exhibited that year, as well as numerous designs for the decorative arts. Haité was for some years President of the Society of Designers, and showed an interest not only in contemporary textiles but in historic aspects of the industry. His publications include 'On the Design and Designers of the Victorian Reign' (*Architectural Review*, II, 1897). The V&A owns a number of his textile designs and
117 fabrics made by Warner & Sons, A. H. Lee and G. P. & J.
9,16 Baker. He also designed textiles for Woollams and for Tomkinson and Adam.

130. George C. **Haité**, photographed by Brown, Barnes & Bell of Baker Street.

Hallward, Reginald (1858–1948) Painter. In 1889, 1893 and 1896 he exhibited designs and embroideries worked by Edith and Henrietta Bloxham and Mary Augusta Smith.

Harris, Jonathan, and Sons Manufacturers and retailers of linen fabrics woven at the Derwent Mill in Cockermouth in the Lake District. They also produced linen embroidery thread. Both products were referred to as 'Harris Flax'. The firm, listed in London from 1877, had shops in Old Bond Street, London; King Street, Manchester; Corporation Street, Birmingham; and in Paris and Berlin. As well as boasting over fifty shades of linen cloth and yarn, Harris also sold *portières*, panels, cushions, screens, and other domestic furnishings worked in appliqué and surface embroidery which used these materials in a variety of artistic and conventional designs. Harris linen fabrics and threads were exhibited in 1889 and 1890 both under the firm's name and by others, including three examples of embroidery worked in Harris Flax thread on Ruskin Linen.

131 **Haslemere Peasant Industries** A community of artist craftsmen set up in Surrey in 1894 in an effort to obtain 'the double pleasure of lovely surroundings and happy work'. Various workshops produced ironwork, pottery, woodwork, fresco painting, hand-press printing, bookbinding, plasterwork and carving, but textiles were by far their most important crafts. The first weaving shed, set up by Mr and Mrs Joseph King in Foundry Meadow, specialized in hand-loom-woven plain and figured materials in linen, cotton and silk. From 1896 their plain fabrics were utilized in appliqué embroideries ('Peasant Tapestries') by Mr and Mrs Godfrey Blount's Peasant Art Society. In 1901 Luther Hooper's Green Bushes Weaving Houses began producing silk, worsted and cotton damasks, brocades, velvets and carpets. One year later, a third weaving company, the St Edmundsbury Weavers, was started by Edmund Hunter. It specialized in luxury silk goods which became popular for church furnishings. The Haslemere Industries employed and trained local women and girls in weaving and embroidery, the aim being 'the revival of a true country life where handicrafts and the arts of husbandry shall exercise body and mind and express the relation of man to earth and to the fruits of earth'. All the Haslemere Industries were frequent participants in the Arts and Crafts and Home Arts and Industries Exhibitions.

131. A workroom at the **Haslemere Peasant Industries** showing the weaving of hand-knotted carpets and embroidery of appliqué hangings.

Haward, Sidney (active 1882–c. 1940) Designer of textiles and wallpapers. He worked at the Silver Studio from 1882 and in 1892 set up the Haward Studio. The Studio began selling designs to G. P. & J. Baker in 1905 and is also known to have had connections with Foxton's and Morton Sundour Fabrics. He exhibited one textile design in 1896, and in 1912 and 1916 showed designs by Hubert and Eric Haward. The V&A owns one carpet design.

† **Heal & Son** Established in 1810 by John Harris Heal as a feather-dressing business. The first premises were in Rathbone Place and in 1818 the business moved to Tottenham Court Road. On John Harris's death in 1833 the business was taken over by his wife and became known as Fanny Heal & Son, shortened to Heal & Son in 1847. Her son, John Harris Heal, Jr, had been a partner since 1834. By 1852 the firm added bedroom furniture to its stock. On John Harris Jr's death in 1876 the business was run by his two sons, Harris and Ambrose, and for the next twenty-six years flourished and expanded to include sitting room furniture and furnishings. Ambrose Heal's son, also called Ambrose (1872–1959), entered the business in 1893 after an apprenticeship as a furniture maker and it is his artistic tastes which influenced the modern development of the shop in the twentieth century. The first furniture catalogue was published in 1898 and about the same time the firm began to advertise the sale of artistic textile furnishings. At the 1900 Paris Exhibition the Heal's stand included Godfrey Blount hangings. The shop also sold printed silk and cotton bedcovers and a wide range of furnishings including printed and woven fabrics by Donald Brothers, Richard Stanway, Turnbull and Stockdale, Newman, Smith and Newman, Warner & Sons, Thomas Wardle, William Foxton, J. H. Dixon, Edmund Hunter, A. H. Lee, G. P. & J. Baker and Alexander Morton. Heal & Son exhibited carpets as part of a room setting in 1903. The V&A owns the archives of the firm, including pattern books and catalogues.

Heaton, John Aldam (1828–97) Designer and decorator. At sixteen he supplied patterns to Halifax textile manufacturers but, frustrated by a lack of success as a designer, he became involved in the trade. His first furnisher's business was in Bradford, with shops eventually opening in many cities in England (from 1877 at 29 Bloomsbury Square). A friend of Norman Shaw, the architect, Heaton was consultant decorator for Bedford Park. His firm also supplied fashionable furnishing fabrics to other retailers, including Morris & Co., who sold Heaton velvets from the late 1860s. He was particularly interested in stencilling and in the 1890s perfected a commercial system for use on textiles. He exhibited one worsted satin in 1896. Other textiles from his designs were shown between 1888 and 1896, including Axminster carpets (Templeton's) and embroideries worked by his wife and daughter. A pair of curtains embroidered by Mrs Mary Newall (a relative of Josephine Mary Newall) was exhibited in 1889. One of these is now in the V&A.

Helbronner, Maison An old-established firm of embroiderers, suppliers of embroidery materials and, from the 1890s, furnishing fabrics. Premises were originally in Regent Street, moving to Oxford Street in 1879. They were represented at the Great Exhibition in 1851 and at the 1889 Arts and Crafts Exhibition they showed a George Fayers embroidery design, three examples of embroidery, and a theatrical costume 'worn by Mr Irving as Macbeth'. The V&A owns an unfinished panel of embroidery bought in the shop in the early twentieth century.

Holiday, Catherine (active from 1875) Embroideress, believed by Morris to be the only one 'whose work is as good as the old'. She worked for Morris & Co. on a commercial basis for a number of years. She embroidered designs by Morris and by her husband, the painter Henry Holiday. These were mostly large-scale bedcovers, hangings and *portières* which were drawn out in Morris & Co.'s workshops and embroidered in the firm's silks. She was a hard-headed businesswoman, and all her work for Morris was done after mutual agreement on colours and materials. He was often worried that her prices of £100–150 per hanging were too high. Three panels embroidered by her, one designed by Morris and another by Henry Holiday, were exhibited in 1888 and 1890. The V&A owns a small collection of Morris silks from her workbag as well as her earliest known embroidered hanging, designed by Morris and made for the Earl of Southampton in 1876.

Hooper, Luther (1849–1932) Designer and weaver. The revival of hand-loom weaving in the twentieth century has been greatly influenced by his teaching and writings. He trained initially as a book illustrator and wood engraver, and his first commercial patterns were for wallpapers. In about 1890 he joined a silk weaving firm in Ipswich (probably the English Silk Weaving Company) where he learned all aspects of the technique. In 1900 he moved to Bushey to superintend a small tapestry weaving studio, and a year later he set up the Green Bushes Weaving Houses at Haslemere with his son and three weavers from Ipswich. He returned to London in 1910 to concentrate on his own work (setting up a studio in Grosvenor Road, Westminster), his teaching and the publication of books on weaving. His *Handloom Weaving, Plain and Ornamental* (1911) is still a standard text. He lectured widely and taught for a number of years at the Central School of Arts and Crafts and at other London County Council establishments. After his retirement in 1923 he continued to write and gave private lessons until his death. He exhibited two Haslemere textiles: a brocaded silk damask in 1903 and a hand-knotted carpet in 1906. The V&A owns several examples of his work.

Horne, Herbert (1864–1916) Writer, architect, designer and member of the Century Guild. He was apprenticed to A. H. Mackmurdo in 1883 and the two were partners 1885–90. He is known to have provided at least one tex-
34 tile design, 'Angel with a Trumpet', for the Guild. In 1890 he moved to Florence to concentrate on art-historical writing. He bequeathed his art collection to Florence, where it is now known as the Museo Horne.

Hunter, Edmund (1866–1937) Designer and weaver. He trained at the Silver Studio and in 1902 set up the St Edmundsbury Weavers at Haslemere, concentrating on the production of hand-loom-woven plain and figured fabrics, mostly worked in silks and woven with gold and other metal threads. His complex early patterns proved particularly suitable for church use. In 1905 Hunter was awarded two gold crosses at the Home Arts and Industries Exhibition for silk and metal hangings. The use of power looms followed a move to Letchworth in 1908 and it was there that Hunter was joined in the business by his son Alec (1899–1958). At Letchworth the firm produced high quality hand- and power-loom-woven silks as well as dress fabrics and silk scarves for Liberty's and lining fabrics for Burberry's. In 1906, whilst still at Haslemere, the company exhibited a hand-tufted rug,
95 but it was not until 1912 and 1916 that its woven fabrics were displayed. The V&A owns a collection of silks designed and made by the Hunters.

Image, Selwyn (1849–1930) Artist, designer and member of the Century Guild. He studied drawing at Oxford under John Ruskin. He was ordained a priest in the Church of England in 1873 but resigned in 1883 to concentrate on his artistic career. He was a contributing member of the Century

132. Selwyn **Image**: 'Proserpine', panel embroidered in silks on linen by Miss J. H. Jones, c. 1890. This is one of the figurative designs sold by the Royal School of Art Needlework.

Guild and from 1888 he produced designs for stained glass
124 and embroidery in his own name. Most of the repeating
patterns sold by the Royal School of Art Needlework in the
1880s and 1890s are his work. He also supplied a series of
132 classical female figures which were incorporated into panels
and screens embroidered in the workshops of the Royal
School. A number of embroideries from his designs by the
Royal School and others were shown in 1889, 1890 and
1896.

Jack, George (1885–1931) Architect and furniture designer. He worked for Philip Webb and eventually became
chief furniture designer at Morris & Co. Embroideries from
his designs were exhibited from 1889 to 1912. These were all
worked by his wife, **Annie Christian Jack** (née Gray), an
accomplished needlewoman and teacher of embroidery at
South Kensington. The V&A owns four panels associated
with the Jack family, which include one worked in wool on
velvet exhibited in 1890 (and a pencil drawing by Hanslip
Fletcher showing the embroidery in the Jacks' Finchley
80 home) and one in silk, taken from a Rossetti engraving,
shown in 1893.

Kay, John Illingworth (1870–1950) Designer. One of the
most important members of the Silver Studio, which he
joined about 1892. He produced book-covers, wallpaper and
textile designs for the Studio before leaving in 1900 to man-
age the stencilling department of the wallpaper firm of Essex
& Co. It is probable that while working there he also provided designs on a free-lance basis, as his name is listed in
G. P. & J. Baker's records. He certainly sold designs to
Morton Sundour, Grafton's and Liberty's. He was a good
amateur watercolourist (he exhibited at the Royal
Academy) and a close friend of Butterfield and Harry Napper. In 1922 he left Essex & Co. and taught part-time at the
Central School of Arts and Crafts. He exhibited two designs
in 1893 and 1896 whilst still a member of the Silver Studio.
The V&A owns several Silver Studio designs and fabrics
26 although only one example by Kay has been identified.

133. J. R. **Kennerley**: watercolour design for a printed textile
manufactured by G. P. & J. Baker c. 1896 for Liberty's. The fabric,
with a matching border, was sold at Bing's Maison de l'Art
Nouveau in Paris, and used for hangings on a cabinet by the French
designer Georges de Feure.

Kennerley, George Randall (active from *c.* 1850) Designer.
He produced a number of designs for woven and printed
textiles at the end of the nineteenth century including work 133
for A. H. Lee, 'cotton tapestries' for Charles Hodges & Co.,
velveteens for John Bennett & Sons and large-scale woven
silks for Warner & Sons. Bennett displayed his work at the
Manchester Arts and Crafts Exhibition of 1895. Examples of
Warner's silks, woven from Kennerley's designs and shown
at the Paris Exhibition of 1900, are now in the V&A.

Keswick School of Industrial Art Founded in 1884 as an
evening institute by Canon and Mrs Hardwicke Rawnsley.
The school specialized in the production of metalwork and
jewellery and exhibited through the Home Arts and Industries Association. A cushion designed and embroidered by
Mrs Rawnsley was shown by the school at the 1889 Arts and
Crafts Exhibition.

In 1888 Miss Twelves moved from Langdale, where she

had helped to establish a spinning and weaving industry, and settled in Keswick. Together with Mrs Rawnsley, she started a similar industry; and John Ruskin agreed to his name being associated with the work. The Keswick Ruskin Linen Industry exhibited spun threads and woven and embroidered pieces in 1889 and 1890. 'Ruskin Linen' and 'Ruskin Lace' are both terms used but the names were also applied to work done in other parts of the Lake District, including Langdale. The V&A owns a sampler worked in 1972–7 from earlier patterns.

King, Jessie Marion (1875–1949) Artist and designer. She trained at Glasgow School of Art and worked as a book illustrator and designer of jewellery, china, wallpaper, woven and printed fabrics, batiks and embroidery. From 1902 she occasionally assisted in the embroidery classes and taught book decoration at the Glasgow School of Art. She was well known for her distinctive clothes, many of which she embroidered herself. In 1902 she won a gold medal at the Turin Exhibition. Her textile designs and embroideries echo her sophisticated yet child-like figurative book illustrations. She provided designs for Alexander Morton who produced printed and woven textiles, some of which were sold through Liberty's. The V&A owns some designs, at least one for textiles.

134

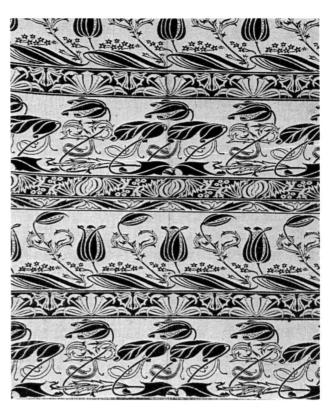

135. Silver Studio (probably Archibald **Knox**): silk and cotton double cloth designed c.1899 and woven in France.

Knox, Archibald (1864–1933) Designer of metalwork and textiles, who worked part-time for the Silver Studio and also sold designs through it. He is now famous for his 'Cymric' silver for Liberty's. Some of his designs are in the Manx Museum at Douglas, Isle of Man; at least one, sold to Richard Stanway, was printed in France. The V&A owns a cotton and silk fabric attributed to him.

135

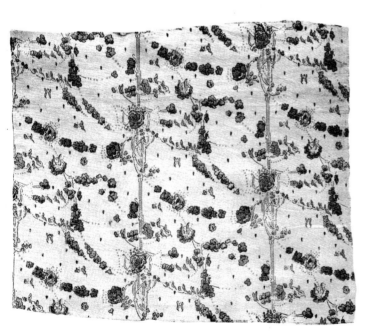

134. Jessie M. **King**: linen printed by Thomas Wardle for Morton Sundour Fabrics, and sold through Heal's, 1908-11.

Ladies' Work Society In 1876 the premises at 31 Sloane Street originally used by the Royal School of Art Needlework were taken by the 'Society for the Sale of Ladies' Work', and the 'Ladies' Work Society' was listed at this address for the first time in 1877. Like the Royal School it was founded to supply employment for impoverished gentlewomen. It advertised secular and church embroidery in all techniques and materials, and also sold patterns, yarns and

136. Mrs Abigail Pepper, manageress of the **Langdale Linen Industry**, 1897.

finished needlework which had first been passed by a selection committee, charging the embroideresses a commission on sales. It exhibited two panels and a cushion worked in silks in 1890.

Langdale Linen Industry Established in 1885 to provide employment in the hamlets of Great and Little Langdale and in nearby Elterwater and Stile, near Coniston and Grasmere in the Lake District. It was begun as a cottage spinning industry by Albert Fleming (who had recently moved into the district) with encouragement from his friend John Ruskin. The collection of old and new spinning wheels (one was copied from a Giotto fresco) was organized by Fleming and his housekeeper, Miss Twelves, and both gave spinning lessons to local people. In 1888 Miss Twelves moved to Keswick and the management was taken over by Mrs Abigail Pepper, a local tiler's wife. Hand-spun and hand-woven linens and some silk and linen dress fabrics were produced at Langdale, but for large quantities of linen sheeting, for

136

instance, the spun yarn was sent for weaving to Scotland. Mrs Pepper also developed vegetable dyeing and embroidery and leading artists were encouraged to provide designs. The Industry utilized historic embroidery techniques, particularly reticella and Greek insertion work, which they called 'Greek Lace'. This term, as well as 'Ruskin Linen' and 'Ruskin Lace', refers to this style of embroidery which was eventually worked throughout the Lake District, but particularly at Langdale and at Keswick under Miss Twelves. In 1893 four cushions designed by Heywood Sumner and embroidered by Mrs Ward were shown. The Langdale Linen Industry was a frequent participant in northern exhibitions, including Lancaster Arts and Crafts, where in 1897 it won fourteen awards.

† **Lee, A. H., & Sons** (also known as Arthur H. Lee & Sons) Manufacturers of woven fabrics. The founder, Arthur Henry Lee (1853–1932), was the son of Henry Lee, one of the first partners in the textile firm of Tootal Broadhurst Lee. At the age of eighteen Arthur was put in charge of the company's spinning mill and later of a cotton mill in Bolton where he set up a few looms to weave patterned woollen cloths. In 1888 he moved his jacquard looms to a corner of Armitage and Rigby's cotton spinning factory in Warrington which was owned by his wife's family. Encouraged by his brother-in-law, G. Faulkner Armitage, who supplied the first designs, Lee began his own business. All the Lee textiles shown at the Arts and Crafts Exhibitions were manufactured in Warrington, although the firm is now best known for its later factory, at Birkenhead, opened in 1904. Lee's produced high quality jacquard-woven wool, silk and cotton furnishing fabrics, using the work of the most important designers of the late nineteenth century including Mackmurdo, Crane, Day, Haité and Voysey. From early experiments with printed warps the firm developed an ingenious technique which involved applying block-printed details to the woven pattern after weaving. Lee's also offered a tapestry and embroidery repair service and *c.* 1905 began to produce large hand-embroidered crewelwork and canvas work curtains and wall panels, as well as small domestic items such as cushion covers and fire-screens. With the move to Birkenhead two of Arthur Lee's sons joined the firm, Christopher eventually becoming a technical expert and Thorold the Design Manager. The third son, Humphrey, started the American firm of Arthur H. Lee Inc. in New York. By 1914 their woven textiles were chiefly reproductions since these had become fashionable. Most designs from this time were drawn in the firm's own studio. Lee's exhibited twelve hangings in 1893 and 1896, using designs by Armitage, Day and Samuel

137. Samuel Rowe: silk and wool double cloth woven by
A. H. **Lee & Sons**, c.1896.

Rowe. They were also present at a number of other exhibitions and supplied textiles for the entrances of the British section of the St Louis Exhibition in 1904. The V&A has designs, point-papers, fabrics and one pattern book obtained when the factory closed in 1970.

Leek Embroidery Society Founded in 1879 or 1880 by Elizabeth Wardle (1834–1902), wife of the printer and dyer Thomas Wardle. The organization benefited from the skills of local Leek embroideresses who had already worked together on various projects. Premises were taken in St Edwards Street (next door to the Wardle family) and a school of embroidery was opened there. Using Wardle fabrics and yarns, embroidery was worked over printed fabrics, including William Morris patterns and printed silks of Indian or Near Eastern design. The Society's individual style was achieved with the use of floss silks and Japanese gold thread. It also produced a great deal of church embroidery worked from designs by a number of architects including Norman Shaw, Gerald Horsley, J. L. Pearson and J. D. Sedding. A copy of the Bayeux Tapestry was embroidered by the Society in 1885–6. In 1888, 1889, 1890 and 1893 the Society exhibited work designed by Thomas Wardle, Jr, and J. D. Sedding. The V&A owns three examples of Leek embroidery.

Lessore, Elaine Thérèse (1884–1945) Designer and embroideress. Sister of Louise and daughter of the artist Jules Lessore. In 1926 she married the painter Walter Sickert (she was his third wife). She exhibited a design for a tapestry chair seat, embroidered costume accessories and furnishings in 1906 and 1910. The V&A owns one embroidered silk panel.

Lessore, Louise (active from 1903) Designer and embroideress. After her marriage to Alfred Powell, an architect and potter, she joined the Cotswold workshops of Gimson and the Barnsleys. She designed and embroidered a frontal for St Andrew's Church, Sunderland. She exhibited five designs for printed muslin in 1903 before her marriage, and under her married name showed embroideries at later exhibitions.

Liberty & Co. Retailers, founded in 1875 by Arthur Lasenby † Liberty (1843–1917) who had previously worked in the Oriental Warehouse of Messrs Farmer and Rogers. The first premises were half a shop at 218A Regent Street called East India House. At first Liberty's concentrated on the sale of imported Eastern goods and occasional exhibitions of historic textiles. Thomas Wardle's printed silks were stocked and the fabrics became so popular that within eighteen months the second half of the premises was bought to cope with this extra trade. By the late 1880s it had become one of the most fashionable shops in London. Departments for carpets, rugs, silks, cretonnes, muslins, 'tapestries' and other furnishings were situated in Chesham House (140–150 Regent Street) with dress fabrics, jewellery, embroideries and Oriental curios at East India House, now extended from 216 to 222 Regent Street. Liberty's purchased furnishing patterns from all the leading designers of the day, including Butterfield, Voysey, Napper, Haité, Mawson, the Silver Studio and Allan Vigers. The fabrics were woven and printed by such firms as Thomas Wardle, G. P. & J. Baker, Turnbull and Stockdale, David Barbour, Alexander Morton and Warner & Sons. Morton was introduced to the shop by Liberty's silk buyer, John Llewellyn, and the association between the two firms proved mutually beneficial. Liberty's were Morton's main English agents and Morton produced a great many fabrics and carpets especially for the shop. A branch was opened in Paris in 1890. At first there was a great deal of resentment from French traders and manufacturers, but soon the shop became very popular, and the high reputation of British textiles abroad dates from this time. Liberty's not only sold British textiles in Europe but also commissioned foreign manufacturers to produce textiles for them. In 1890, 1899 and 1903 they exhibited a hand-tufted carpet

113

designed by Voysey (now in the V&A) and four Morton woven fabrics designed by Voysey, Gavin Morton and J. S. Rigby. The V&A owns a large collection of Liberty's catalogues, woven and printed textiles, carpets and embroideries as well as other textiles which may have been sold by them originally.

Liverpool School of Art The embroidery department was started in 1902 by the school's Principal, F. V. Burridge. At first no technical instruction was given, the students receiving only design tuition from Burridge and Mr Baxter, the school's Master of Design. Freely worked, experimental embroideries resulted which show the influence of work done in Birmingham and Glasgow. Gwendoline Parry, Fanny Pickering, Helena Shaw, Florence Laverick and Frances Jones were the most celebrated embroideresses and Frances Jones went on to work at the Royal School of Art Needlework.

33 **Macbeth, Ann** (1875–1948) Designer and one of the most influential embroideresses of the period. She trained at the Glasgow School of Art and in 1901, while still a student, was asked to assist Jessie Newbery in her embroidery classes. Her work was shown as part of the Glasgow Section of the Turin Exhibition of 1902 and singled out for special notice in *The Studio.* In the same year she was awarded the top prize in her class in the International *Studio* Exhibition. She was a prolific designer and drew out many embroideries for her students and friends. She designed for Liberty's, Donald Brothers of Dundee, and the Knox Linen Thread Company. She published embroidery books, including *Educational Needlecraft* with Margaret Swanson (1911) in which they advocated new ways of teaching needlework in schools, many of which were adopted. She took over as head of embroidery at Glasgow School of Art in 1908 on Jessie Newbery's retirement and taught there until 1928. She retired to Patterdale in the Lake District where she continued to embroider and to teach local women. She exhibited embroideries she had designed in 1903, 1906 and 1916. The
83 V&A owns an embroidered curtain, a tablecloth, and an
32 embroidered picture designed by her.

Macclesfield School of Embroidery Founded by J. O. Nicholson, a leading Macclesfield silk manufacturer. By

1898 it was described as 'one of the foremost' embroidery establishments. The school's reputation was made with embroideries worked on woven silk probably manufactured in Nicholson's Hope Mill, which he opened in 1887. Other items used a ground of linen specially woven on a wide loom so that coverlets could be made without seams. Conventional floral designs were favoured although more adventurous patterns were supplied by G. F. Armitage. The V&A owns an embroidered coverlet.

Mackintosh, Charles Rennie (1868–1928) Architect, designer and watercolour artist, one of the most influential figures in twentieth-century European design. He attended evening classes at Glasgow School of Art and, as the protégé of Francis Newbery, the Principal, was chosen in 1896 to design a new building for the school which he completed in 1909. By that time his work was internationally known through exhibitions in Vienna in 1900, Turin in 1902 and various other European venues. Although he and his wife, Margaret Macdonald, designed various textile accessories for the houses that he built, these are very plain, to suit the architecture. His interest in textile patterns for their own sake came much later in his career. Having given up architecture, he and his wife moved to London, and while there, *c.* 1915–23, he earned a living designing repeating patterns for William Foxton and Sefton's Ltd. Very little, however, has been positively identified as his work. His only textile exhibit with the Arts and Crafts Society was a stencilled canvas back on a settle shown in 1896. The V&A 69 owns a few designs, two printed fabrics, and a lampshade 84 panel embroidered by Margaret Macdonald.

Mackmurdo, Arthur Heygate (1851–1942) Architect and 45 designer, founder member of the Century Guild in 1882 and of the Arts and Crafts Exhibition Society. He set up as an architect in 1875, and from 1885 worked in partnership with Herbert Horne. Mackmurdo designed most of the repeating textiles for the Century Guild. He was a close friend of William Morris, and it is likely that some Century Guild wall rugs were made at Merton Abbey. In the 1880s he encouraged another friend, Voysey, to become a designer. His patterns were shown as part of the Century Guild's exhibits in 63 1888. Although there is no substantive evidence that he continued to design textiles after the Guild disbanded in 1888, it is likely that an embroidered screen exhibited by 'Mackmurdo and Horne' in 1889 was designed by him, and examples of woven fabrics by A. H. Lee and Warner & Sons are likely to be of a later date. The V&A collection of embroidery and woven and printed textiles by the Century

138. Sidney **Mawson**: 'Chatsworth', roller-printed cotton registered in December 1909. Manufactured by Turnbull and Stockdale for Liberty's, who have sold the design throughout the twentieth century.

60,61 Guild contains at least five patterns known to be by Mack-murdo.

Mawson, Sidney (active from 1882, d. 1941) Landscape painter and designer of wallpapers and textiles. He was for a time a lecturer at the Slade School. He had a very long career as a designer and remained commercially successful by changing his style to suit fashions and the individual tastes of manufacturers. His first known textile designs, for Thomas

30 Wardle in the early 1880s, follow Morris's work quite closely but by the end of the century he drew more stylized floral designs in vogue at that time. Within a few years he had

138 begun to produce naturalistic patterns in bright colours and these proved to be his most individual and successful work. Much of his later work was printed by Morton Sundour Fabrics and sold through Liberty's. One design, 'Pleasaunce', was the printer's most popular pattern. Mawson sold designs to many other leading British manufacturers, including G. P. & J. Baker, Thomas Wardle, Warner & Sons, Alexander Morton and Turnbull and Stockdale. He exhibited two cottons in 1888 and one cretonne in 1896 which, although not

listed in the catalogue, was illustrated in the *Art Journal*. The V&A owns a representative collection of his designs and textiles including some silks woven by Warner's used at Charlottenburg Palace, Berlin.

Millar, Cecil (active from *c.* 1900) Designer of interiors, furniture, wallpapers and textiles. Whereas his early designs are eclectic, by 1905 he had developed an individual style showing modern geometric designs in bright colours based on the motifs of European peasant decoration. Within a few years he had returned to a less original style influenced by historic patterns. He drew designs for woven and printed textiles and carpets and sold these to G. P. & J. Baker, Warner & Sons, Thomas Wardle, William Foxton, Alexander Morton, Turnbull and Stockdale, and the London shops of Liberty's, Story's, John Wilson and Heal's. Millar's textiles exhibited in 1903 and 1906 included fabrics printed by

89 G. P. & J. Baker, Wardle and Turnbull and Stockdale, a carpet shown by John Wilson and textiles woven by Alexander Morton and Warner & Sons. The V&A owns designs and one carpet woven for Story's in 1906.

Morris, Jane (1839–1914) Embroideress. She married William Morris in 1859 and her first embroideries were made for the Red House built for them by Philip Webb in 1860. It is said that she was taught to embroider by her husband although she is likely to have been an experienced needlewoman before they met. She adopted his favourite technique of woollen embroidery in her early work which was chiefly intended for wall panels, with floral and figurative designs drawn by Morris. She continued to embroider 81 throughout her life and, in later years, copied several designs by her younger daughter, May. She exhibited six embroideries between 1888 and 1916, including a *portière* designed by Morris and worked by Jane and her elder daughter Jenny in 1888, a tablecloth and cot cover designed by May in 1890, and a cross-stitch panel and white embroidered dress in 1916. The V&A owns a bag and a bell-pull worked by her.

Morris, Jenny (Jane Alice) (1861–1935) Elder daughter of William and Jane Morris. In 1876 she developed epilepsy and had to abandon a promising education. She spent the rest of her life as an invalid and embroidery appears to have been one of her main occupations. She exhibited some embroideries worked by herself and others made with her mother and sister. The latter included a case containing embroidery, bead necklaces and jewellery, worked by Jenny and May, shown in 1899.

Morris, May (Mary) (1862–1938) Younger daughter of William and Jane Morris. She attended Notting Hill High School and the South Kensington Schools. From 1885 to c. 1896 she managed the embroidery section of Morris & Co. and supervised much of the work from her own drawing room at Hammersmith Terrace. After the breakup of her marriage and her extended absence abroad following her father's death in 1896, she concentrated on her own needlework, publications and the teaching of embroidery. She was very interested in technique and her first article, 'Chain Stitch Embroidery', for the Century Guild's magazine *Hobby Horse*, was published in 1888. In 1892 she contributed a chapter on embroidery to Mackmurdo's book *Plain Handicraft* and in the following year published her Arts and Crafts essays and the first of a series of articles on ecclesiastical embroidery for the *Building News*. Her most authoritative book was *Decorative Needlework* (1893). She taught at the Central School of Arts and Crafts 1897–1907 and took over Mary Newill's class at Birmingham for a time. She lectured at a number of British art schools and her influence can be seen in the work of embroideresses such as Grace Christie. One of her notable achievements was the establishment in 1907 of the Women's Guild of Art. Her own work is best known through the panels, wall hangings and bedcovers made for Morris & 79 Co., many of which she designed. Her private work also used 81 her own designs and those of artist friends but is more delicate in colouring and detail. She took part in all the Arts and Crafts Exhibitions, showing work done for Morris & Co. and some in her maiden name and also as Mrs Sparling. The 'Fruit Tree' hanging shown in 1890 is her finest and most characteristic design for the firm. She also showed embroideries designed by her father, Philip Webb, and Charles Ricketts. In 1916 the Women's Guild of Art submit- 72 ted a lady's bedroom with hangings designed by her. She is well represented in the V&A by a few designs and embroideries ranging from Morris & Co. hangings to small domestic items intended for her own use, many bequeathed by her.

Morris, William (1834–1896) Artist and designer, the †️ greatest single influence on the Arts and Crafts Movement and the most successful textile designer and manufacturer of his day. He became interested in all aspects of textile technique, first as an amateur and eventually as a commercial manufacturer. Together with Thomas Wardle, he revived block-printing and vegetable dyeing and in his own home set up looms for tapestry weaving and the hand knotting of carpets. Morris had the innate gift of being able to draw successful original designs quickly. He was highly influenced by historical patterns and was one of the most knowledgeable textile historians of the late nineteenth century, acting for a time as an art referee for proposed acquisitions by the Textiles Department of the South Kensington Museum. He designed all Morris & Co. embroideries, woven and printed textiles and carpets until the mid-1880s when he became interested in other activities. He was involved in the Arts and Crafts Society from the beginning and was an early Committee member but was sceptical at first that its aims could be fulfilled. He became President in 1893. His work was shown at all the exhibitions and a retrospective display was held in 1899. The V&A owns a number of his original designs and has the world's largest public collection of his textiles, with examples of all techniques including most of his printed and woven patterns.

Morris & Co. Founded by William Morris in 1875, the firm †️ eventually produced embroideries, printed and woven textiles, carpets and tapestries for sale at their shops in Queen Square, in Oxford Street (1877–1917), and in George Street, Hanover Square. Before the opening of the Merton Abbey Works in 1881 other manufacturers produced textiles

139. J. H. Dearle for **Morris & Co.**: 'The Pigeon', *portière*, c.1890. Embroidered by Mrs Battye with silks on a background of 'Oak' silk damask manufactured by the firm.

for the firm. These included Thomas Wardle, J. O. Nicholson of Macclesfield, H. C. McCrea of Halifax and Dixon of Bradford. Alexander Morton provided silk and wool fabrics and gauzes, while machine-woven carpets were made at Wilton and by the Heckmondwike Manufacturing Company. From 1885 May Morris ran the embroidery section of the company and J. H. Dearle, Morris's assistant, increasingly directed the production of other textiles. Dearle was also responsible for most of the designs from this period and supervised schemes for house decoration. Dearle took over management of the firm on Morris's death in 1896 and in 1905 was appointed Art Director under a Board of Directors. At this time the company opened a workshop for the cleaning and repair of tapestries. Morris's designs continued to be sold but Dearle changed his own style to suit prevailing fashions. Despite this, Morris & Co. never regained its early commercial success. The Merton Abbey Works closed during the First World War. They re-opened in 1920 and continued to manufacture a range of textiles although production was limited. The firm eventually went into liquidation in 1940. Morris & Co. were enthusiastic participants in all the Arts and Crafts Exhibitions, showing a great number of objects. The V&A's holding is large and includes designs, cartoons, tracings, and all forms of textiles.

† **Morton, Alexander, & Co.** Founded by Alexander Morton (1844–1923) on the basis of the local muslin industry in Darvel, Scotland. He began in 1867 by employing several weavers to produce woven lenos in their homes. He improved the quality of the fabrics which he supplied to Glasgow shops and was soon selling to English traders including Swan and Edgar's and Shoolbred's in London. In 1870 Alexander went into partnership with his brother Robert and his cousin, also called Alexander Morton. The monopoly of Nottingham machine-made lace in the British market persuaded the partners that power-loom weaving had to be adopted and in 1881 they opened a factory with twenty-four lace looms. Plain chenilles for curtains were the first heavy fabrics made by the firm and many redundant hand-loom weavers were employed. The production of heavy-weight woollen fabrics and three-ply carpeting followed and by the mid–1890s the weaving of double cloths made from mixtures of silk and wool and cotton and wool had started. In 1896 Morton visited Ireland and was asked to help provide work in poverty-stricken Donegal. He opened his first carpet factory in Killybegs in 1898, followed by others in Kilcar and Gweedore. These hand-knotted 'Donegal' carpets are characterized by particularly bright colours, especially orange-pinks and greens. In 1895 the

140, 141. Woven fabrics by Alexander **Morton** & Co. *Top*, cotton and wool textile from the 'Flora' range, possibly designed by J. Nichol, who produced other patterns for the firm. *Above*, section of a cotton cloth; similar items appear in Liberty's catalogue *1901 Yuletide Gifts* where they are called 'Drawing Room (or Boudoir) Table covers'.

partnership was dissolved and the firm's management came under Alexander Morton's two eldest sons, James and Guy, with his nephew Gavin Morton running the design studio. The firm bought a disused mill in Carlisle in 1900 and transferred all but gauze weaving to this factory. James Morton (1867–1943) encouraged the production of new fabrics and was responsible for buying work from most of the leading free-lance designers of the day. The firm had contracts with Voysey and Butterfield and also produced fabrics from the designs of Day, Mawson, Napper, the Silver Studio, J. S. Rigby, Cecil Millar, Harrison Townsend, Baillie Scott, Frederick Vigers and many others. Morton's provided all the largest British shops with gauzes, woven fabrics and carpets. It became one of the main suppliers to Wylie and Lochhead in Glasgow and Liberty's, and also supplied carpets to Maple's and double cloths and gauzes to Morris & Co. Alexander Morton exhibited frequently from 1896 and showed Donegal carpets, chenille curtains, Madras muslins, woven woollen 'tapestries' and double cloths. From 1905 Morton's included printed textiles in their range and in 1906 these were transferred to a new company, **Morton Sundour Fabrics**. At first printing was undertaken by other British and foreign firms but by 1912 Morton Sundour had their own unit. The V&A has a large collection of designs and woven and printed fabrics and carpets from both the Morton firms, many of which were given by Alexander Morton's great-grandson, Jocelyn. An exhibition, *The Mortons*, was held at the Museum in 1973.

Morton, Gavin (1867–1954) Eldest son of Robert Morton, who was the elder brother and early partner of Alexander Morton. When the partnership between Robert and Alexander Morton broke up in 1895 Gavin stayed with his uncle's firm as chief designer. He had extensive technical and commercial knowledge learned from representing the firm on trips around Britain which helped to make him a very successful textile designer. (He had also visited America in 1893 with his cousin, James Morton.) His repeating patterns are often mistaken for Voysey's but his style is simpler, using larger areas of flat colour which suited Morton's production of machine- and hand-made carpets and the technique of silk and wool double cloth. In the early twentieth century he perfected a new carpet loom at Carlisle, and, in 1908, he took the patent for this to start a new carpet business, Blackwood, Morton, in Kilmarnock. A few of Gavin Morton's textiles were exhibited by Alexander Morton in 1896 and 1899. These included carpets, woven woollen fabrics, silk and wool and silk and chenille double cloths. The V&A have some examples of his work.

142. Harry **Napper**:'Hemlock', 1899, the first design he sold to G. P. & J. Baker after leaving the Silver Studio. Baker's printed the design on both cotton and velveteen.

Napper, Harry (1860–1940) Watercolour painter and † designer of furniture, metalwork, wallpapers and textiles. He joined the Silver Studio *c.* 1893 and managed design production there after Arthur Silver's death in 1896. He left in 1898 to work on a free-lance basis but continued to sell patterns through the Studio for a few years. He absorbed the most fashionable elements of British and Continental design at the end of the century and produced a range of highly successful, very eccentric, stylized floral designs. He sold his work to many manufacturers, including G. P. & J. Baker, Turnbull and Stockdale, and Alexander Morton and also to French manufacturers, with whom his work was particularly popular. He exhibited only one design, for a woven fabric, which was shown in 1899, his first year as a free-lance designer. The V&A have several of his original designs and textiles, most made while he was at the Silver Studio.

Newall, Josephine Mary (active from the 1880s, d. 1923) Embroideress. She was already an accomplished needlewoman and keen teacher before she moved to Fisherton-de-la-Mare in 1902 and set up the Fisherton Industry, where embroidery was worked by local men and women. This

143. Jessie **Newbery**, wearing artistically embroidered clothing of the Scottish type illustrated in *Moderne Stickereien*, published in Darmstadt in 1905.

concentrated on white cotton embroidery, with historical patterns as the main source for designs. From 1907 the Fisherton Industry became a member of the Home Arts and Industries Association and frequently exhibited at the Albert Hall. Mrs Newall did not exhibit any of her Fisherton embroideries with the Arts and Crafts Society until 1916, when she showed domestic items (sideboard cloth, tea cloth, cushion covers and a sofa back). Her relative, Mrs Mary Newall, was also an embroideress (see Heaton). The V&A owns three designs and a large, very competently worked bedcover designed by Mrs Newall and embroidered at Fisherton in 1908.

143 **Newbery, Jessie** (1864–1948) Designer and embroideress. The daughter of a Paisley shawl manufacturer, she attended Glasgow School of Art. In 1889 she married the Principal, Francis H. Newbery (1853–1946). In 1894 she began to teach embroidery there, offering tuition to full- and part-time students and to teachers on Saturdays. At first she taught crewelwork similar to the styles and techniques made popular by Morris and the Royal School of Art Needlework but within a year or two she had developed her own style using appliqué with heavy linen and cotton fabrics and a minimum of stitching. She believed that this rather experimental method would result in more imaginative work and her ideas were taken into school teaching by a student, Ann Macbeth, who eventually took over her class in 1908. Her characteristic motif of a circular rose influenced many members of the Glasgow School and her lettering, seen in the inscriptions of a number of her embroideries, also became popular with her students. Although much of her work was published in *The Studio*, as with other Glasgow designers her reputation during her own lifetime was greater abroad than in Britain. She exhibited in 1893, 1896 and 1899. The V&A has five of her embroideries: two collars, one with matching belt, and two cushions. 82,85

Newill, Mary J. (1860–1947) Painter, book illustrator, embroideress and designer of textiles and stained glass. She attended Birmingham School of Art and trained under E. R. Taylor. While she was there she won a travelling scholarship which enabled her to spend a year studying in Paris. She returned to teach embroidery at the school 1892–1920, except for a short break when she studied tempera painting in Florence while May Morris took over her class. She was a member of the Bromsgrove Guild of Applied Arts and directed all their embroidery. She designed ecclesiastical furnishings and several embroideries were worked from her designs by students. She is now best known for her use of appliqué techniques influenced by stained glass and especially by woodcuts. Her finest designs are large figurative panels worked in appliqué, usually with woollen embroidery instead of the more familiar silk and linen used by the Glasgow embroideresses. She exhibited examples of needlework between 1893 and 1916, including the *Faerie Queene* set, worked by the Bromsgrove Guild, in 1899, and an embroidered picture, 'Gareth and Lynet', in 1903. The V&A owns the latter, and also a set of four embroidered curtains and pelmets worked in 1906 in wools on linen which combine to make a landscape. 73 74

Obrist, Hermann (1863–1927) Swiss-born architect, sculptor and highly influential Jugendstil designer, who trained in Heidelberg and Karlsruhe. His 'whiplash' embroideries are seen as some of the most significant manifestations of Continental Art Nouveau. He designed many embroideries and in 1892 opened an embroidery workshop in Florence which he moved to Munich in 1894. He was one of the few foreign exhibitors at the Arts and Crafts Exhibitions and the only one who neither lived nor traded in Britain. In 1896 he showed six embroideries and one hearth rug. All these were made by Berthe Ruchet who was the Director of his Munich *atelier*. It is probably that the embroideries illustrated in *The Studio* for 1896 were exhibition pieces.

Pattison, Edgar L. (active from 1896) Decorative painter and designer of wallpapers, furniture, costumes and textiles. He was a member of the Society of Designers. He sold work to G. P. & J. Baker, Charles Hodges & Co. and the French manufacturers Vanoutryve et Cie. Other textiles were sold through Liberty's. Embroidery patterns drawn by him for collars, cuffs and revers were published in the *Art Workers' Quarterly* for 1902. He exhibited designs for printed textiles in 1896 and 1899 and a printed silk in 1906.

Pesel, Louisa (1870–1947) Designer and embroideress who trained under Lewis F. Day. She assisted W. G. Paulson Townsend with his book *Embroidery or the Craft of the Needle* (1899), in which two of her embroideries are illustrated. She left Day's studio in 1900 but by that time had begun to exhibit her own work. A screen shown in the First International *Studio* Exhibition received special attention. In 1902 she was appointed designer to the Royal Hellenic Schools of Needlework and Lace in Athens and it was while she was there that she studied historic and modern embroideries from the area. She became Director of the school but left Greece in 1907 to return to England. In about 1910 she was commissioned by the V&A to produce a set of stitch samplers based on English embroidery of the seventeenth and eighteenth centuries. These were published in 1911. In 1913 a second series based on embroideries of the Mediterranean and the Near East were also published. Both sets of samplers are on permanent display at the V&A, which also owns a panel adapted from one of her published designs. A keen technician and teacher of embroidery, she

144. Edgar **Pattison**: 'Strawberry and Grape', watercolour design for printed linen manufactured by G. P. & J. Baker in 1906, sold through Heal's.

became an Inspector of Art Needlework for the Board of Education and the first President of the Embroiderers' Guild in 1920. Her mature work was based on the revival of historic designs and techniques, and embroideries copied from her stitch sampler books are often thought to be Greek or Near Eastern.

Reuter, Edmond G. (1845–after 1912) Swiss-born artist and designer of ceramics, textiles and illuminated manuscripts. He trained as a textile designer in Paris and Mulhouse and at South Kensington, then worked for twenty years as a ceramic designer for Minton's. In later life he returned to his native Geneva and produced hand-painted 'tapestry' hangings. Three photographs of these were exhibited in 1890.

Reynolds-Stephens, Annie (active from 1893) Embroideress. A frequent exhibitor between 1893 and 1916, she embroidered designs by Voysey and by her husband, the sculptor and craftsman, William Reynolds-Stephens (1862–1943).

Rigby, George R. (active by 1895) Stenciller and designer of wallpapers and textiles. Worked first in the Chapel Studio, Leek, and then at Uttoxeter. He is best known as a wallpaper designer, and wrote an article on stencilling for the *Art Workers' Quarterly* in 1902. Several of his embroidery designs were illustrated in contemporary magazines and one panel, worked by his sister, was shown at the Chester Arts and Crafts Exhibition of 1902. He sold designs to 91 G. P. & J. Baker and a number of these are still owned by the company. He exhibited a design for a machine-printed cretonne in 1896 and in the same year showed two textile designs at the Manchester Arts and Crafts Exhibition.

Rigby, John Scarratt (active by 1889) Designer. Possibly part of the company 'Rigby and Rigby' which exhibited machine-printed muslin curtains, designed by 'John Rigby', in 1889. A founder member of the Society of Designers, he wrote a number of reviews and articles on design including 'Remarks on Morris Work and its Influence on British Decorative Arts of To-Day' (*Art Workers' Quarterly*, 1902). He produced designs for G. P. & J. Baker and Alexander Morton and his woven and printed textiles were sold through Liberty's. In 1890 and 1893 he exhibited designs for velvets and in 1899 a silk and cotton double cloth made by Morton and sold through Liberty's. The V&A owns two 92 designs and one printed cotton.

Rooke, Thomas Matthew (1842–1942) Painter and assistant in Edward Burne-Jones's studio. In 1888 three narrative panels based on the legend of the Golden Fleece designed by

him and embroidered by Emma Lucy Jones were exhibited and in 1889 a needlework panel by him was shown by the same embroideress.

Rowe, Samuel (active from *c.* 1888) Designer. He showed a design for a Music Room at the 1890 Manchester Arts and Crafts Exhibition, and because entries for this exhibition were restricted he is likely to have been based in the North of England. His only known textile designs are those sold to A. H. Lee and Turnbull and Stockdale. Lee's exhibited 1,137 three examples at the 1896 Arts and Crafts Exhibition. The V&A owns two Lee woven fabrics and a matching point-paper.

Royal School of Art Needlework Founded in 1872 as the School of Art Needlework with premises in Sloane Street. In 1875 it moved to dilapidated buildings in Exhibition Road erected for the 1862 International Exhibition. It was granted the prefix 'Royal' through the patronage of Queen Victoria's daughter, Princess Christian of Schleswig-Holstein, its first President. Started with the dual purpose of improving the standard of commercial embroidery and 'providing suitable employment for educated women', the school became the foremost embroidery establishment in Britain and a model for similar organizations abroad. Showing a wide range of styles and techniques, in its early years it used designs by Morris, Burne-Jones, Crane and G. F. Bodley. It was awarded medals at both the Philadelphia Centennial Exposition of 1876 and the Paris Exhibition of 1878. These helped to secure its success. In the 1880s and 1890s it commissioned work from many other popular designers, including Selwyn Image and W. G. Paulson Townsend, who became Art 124 Director. It started its own studio which was run for a time by Nellie Wichelo, who also provided many designs. Under the management of a Miss Wade the school undertook all types of religious, domestic and ceremonial embroidery. It also offered a cleaning and repair service for embroideries and tapestries. One- and two-year courses were offered in various techniques, including hand and frame embroidery, crewelwork, canvas work, silk embroidery, appliqué and 'ecclesiastical work'. There were evening classes and special training courses for professional embroideresses and teachers, many attending from art schools throughout England. In 1903 the school moved into large purpose-built premises in Exhibition Road designed by Fairfax Wade, an architect who also supplied designs for embroidery. The patronage by Royalty and aristocracy assured commercial success and the school was responsible for the embroidery of furnishings for many ceremonial occasions. Another lucra-

145. Walter Crane: three panels from a five-fold screen embroidered by the **Royal School of Art Needlework** in wools on a satin ground. Representing the elements, with inscriptions taken from Theocritus, the screen was shown at the Philadelphia Centennial Exposition in 1876.

tive business was the sale of embroidery materials and designs and many of these have survived as embroideries worked by amateurs. A great many of the Royal School's embroideries were exhibited by the school itself, by designers and by amateurs working from kits. The V&A owns a number of embroideries worked at the school. Designers represented are Morris, Burne-Jones (the panel 'The Mill' is on loan to

132

Wightwick Manor), Crane, Fairfax Wade and Alexander Fisher.

145

Royal Windsor Tapestry Company Founded in 1876 by H. C. J. Henry, an interior decorator and artistic adviser to Gillow & Co. Henry persuaded M. Brignolas and six weavers from the French Aubusson factory to start a tapestry works in

Windsor. From temporary accommodation, in 1882 they moved to purpose-built workshops on nearby Crown land and the company was officially designated 'Royal'. The factory produced a number of sets of tapestries of which the most celebrated, 'The Merry Wives of Windsor', commissioned by Gillows, was awarded a gold medal at the Paris Exhibition of 1878. The company exhibited a design and tapestry of 'King Alfred in the Danish Camp' by Herbert Bone in 1888. Their products were too expensive for most households and when royal commissions stopped the works closed in 1895. The V&A owns what is probably their first tapestry, a portrait of Queen Victoria after Heinrich von Angeli, woven in 1877, and also a set of cartoons for 'Royal Residences'.

Scott, M. H. Baillie (1865–1945) One of the most highly regarded and original architects of the late nineteenth and early twentieth centuries, and also a designer of furniture and textiles. He was very influential abroad, and his work at Darmstadt for the Duke of Hesse is one of the major architectural and design projects of the period. He used embroidery (particularly appliqué) to decorate the textiles in 77 his interiors. He set out his views in 'Some Experiments in Embroidery' (*The Studio*, 1903). Panels for a screen designed 78 by him and embroidered by his wife were exhibited in 1896 and are now in the V&A, together with an embroidered collar.

Sedding, John Dando (1838–91) Church architect who trained in G. E. Street's office where he met Philip Webb and Morris. He was a significant designer of church furnishings, and his extant work includes several fine embroidered altar frontals. He was a keen early member of the Arts and Crafts Society. In 1888, 1889 and 1890 he showed a design, two embroideries (one worked by Rose Sedding, the other by the Leek Embroidery Society), and a silk printed by Thomas Wardle.

100 **Silver, Arthur** (1853–96) Designer. The son of an upholsterer and cabinet maker, he attended Reading School of Art 1869–72. He was then apprenticed to the furniture, wallpaper and textile designer H. W. Batley, where he learned the rudiments of textile techniques. In 1880 he started the Silver Studio and for the next ten years produced a great range of repeating designs, selling these at first to manufacturers and shops he had got to know while working in Batley's studio. His early patterns are varied and eclectic, reflecting the influence of Morris and other established designers. His main source for ideas was the South Kensington Museum and while he was very interested in Japanese ornament his work also shows elements of other styles. One of Silver's earliest original designs was the 'Peacock Feather' sold to Liberty's and printed for them by the Rossendale Printing Company in 1888. His mature work is very stylish, and in an article on Rottman & Co. wallpaper stencils in *The Studio* for 1895 Gleeson White praised Silver's use of colour. The Silver Studio's work increased greatly between 1890 and 1896 and when Silver died he was at the peak of his career. Although a number of his designs can be recognized, his work is inextricably linked with the Studio he founded. His influence there, seen in its efficient management and the variety of work produced, cannot be overestimated. He was friendly with many leading members of the Arts and Crafts Movement and took an active interest in the Society's events, exhibiting designs in his own name in 1890, 1893 and 1896.

Silver Studio Started in 1880 by Arthur Silver at Brook † Green, moving later to Haarlem Road, Hammersmith. Founded for the production of repeating designs for furnishing fabrics, wallpapers and floor coverings, it also sold patterns for plasterwork, dress fabrics, stencils, metalwork, furniture, book jackets, advertisements and trade cards. Its 'Silvern Series' of photographs of historic textiles from the V&A became a lucrative sideline. Two of Arthur Silver's sons, Reginald (Rex) and Harry, joined the Studio, and on their father's premature death Rex (1879–1965) took over as Business Manager although he was only seventeen. Harry Napper served as Design Manager until he left in 1898. In 1900 Rex took full control with help from his younger brother, Harry (1882–1972), who by this time had trained under Napper and J. I. Kay, the Studio's two most outstanding designers in the late nineteenth century. Harry Silver's designs are less obviously Art Nouveau than those of Napper or Kay but his work while Artistic Director, from the early years of the twentieth century until 1916, moulded the Silver Studio's very successful style. Other notable figures were associated with the Studio, including the Manxman Archibald Knox, whose interest in Celtic design is thought to have influenced its strong Art Nouveau style. The list of clients who bought designs is immense and includes all the leading British textile manufacturers of the late nineteenth

146. **Silver Studio**: cotton fabric, woven in France by Leborgne of Lannoy from Silver Studio design 13638, sold to the company in May 1906.

and twentieth centuries. Among these were Daniel Lee & Co., Templeton & Co., Swaisland Printing Co., Warner & Sons, Stead McAlpin, Schwabe & Co., Newman, Smith and Newman, Liberty's, F. Steiner, Alexander Morton, A. H. Lee, Brinton's, Whittall's, Tomkinson and Adam and G. P. & J. Baker. The Studio's work was particularly popular abroad: in 1898, 62 designs were sold to French manufacturers, and in 1906, 64 were bought by Leborgne of Lille alone. From 1914 American firms also became clients. The V&A owns a collection of woven and printed fabrics made from Silver Studio designs given in 1969 by Mary Peerless, Rex Silver's stepdaughter. The Studio's records, library, and unsold designs were given by Miss Peerless to Middlesex Polytechnic.

Sleath, William (active from *c.* 1880) Tapestry weaver. He joined Morris & Co. and became one of the first two tapestry apprentices to be taught by J. H. Dearle at Queen Square and, from 1881, at Merton Abbey. He was a master weaver with the firm until the First World War and worked on its most important tapestries, including 'Peace' shown in 1889 and 'The Forest' shown in 1890. While working at Morris & Co. he undertook tapestry conservation and wove designs privately. Four of the latter were exhibited between 1896 and 1912; the designers of three of these were identified as Innes Fripp, Maud Beddington and J. D. Batten. He also wove a copy of the Fra Angelico *predella* from San Domenico in Fiesole (National Gallery, London) which is now in Winchelsea Church.

Solon, Léon Victor (1872–1957) Art director and chief designer at Minton's. Although a few of his textile designs were illustrated in contemporary magazines only one existing example, a figurative design printed by Thomas Wardle, is known. This is similar to his patterns for pottery and particularly tiles, which often show fashionable female figures in the style of Alphonse Mucha.

Southall, Joseph (1861–1944) Artist and designer. He was articled to a leading firm of architects in Birmingham but after attending evening classes at Birmingham School of Art became interested in the applied arts. One of the leading decorative painters of the 'Birmingham School', he also produced book illustrations and a few designs for textiles. All of these were worked in the popular cut-work and insertion technique of 'Greek Lace' and embroidered on Langdale Linen by his mother, Elizabeth Maria Southall. It is possible that it was Mrs Southall rather than the designer himself who chose the technique. Two panels, an apron, a workbag,

147. Heywood **Sumner**: woollen fabric woven by Alexander Morton c. 1900, probably 'Colour and Leaf Colonnade'.

a nightdress case and a fire-screen – all with attractive floral and figurative designs – were shown between 1893 and 1906.

Spinnery, The: see Garnett, Annie

Spitalfields Silk Association An organization which exhibited two woven silks, both designed by Aymer Vallance, in 1896. About the same time it sponsored an exhibition with the English Silk Weaving Company.

Stanway, Richard (active 1870s–1905) Retailer. In July 1878 Stanway became a partner of Benjamin Warner and Charles Ramm and for a year the firm traded as Warner, Ramm & Stanway. He then left to form his own business, buying and selling furnishing fabrics. From 1880 he traded as a warehouseman from premises at 2 King Edward Street, London, where he remained until 1905. Advertisements show a wide range of goods for sale: cretonnes, printed velveteens, Vandyke silk velvets, Chenonceau velvets, brocatelles, Sicilian silks and guipure laces. These were sold from his shop and by representatives travelling throughout Britain. He bought patterns from most of the leading textile designers, including Voysey, and his name appears frequently in the records of the Silver Studio. He commissioned manufacturers to print and weave designs to sell under his own name (and registered a number of these patterns) and also re-sold designers' work to other shops and manufacturers. The records of foreign firms indicate that he 101 supplied designs to them, and it is likely that in the case of Gros Roman of Mulhouse these were then sold back to Liberty's. Various reports on Stanway in *Furniture and Decoration* suggest that he was a leading supplier in the 1890s.

Sumner, Heywood (1853–1940) Designer, archaeologist, painter and etcher. He exhibited at the Royal Academy 1880–83 and was associated with the Century Guild from 1884. A specialist in sgraffito work, he also designed stained 147 glass, textiles and wallpapers. Alexander Morton used his patterns and a tapestry, 'The Chase', was woven by Morris & Co. in 1908. He designed several ecclesiastical embroideries, including a banner of St Michael for Malvern Priory. A number of his embroideries were exhibited: in 1890 'Earth, Air, Fire and Water', embroidered by Mary Augusta Smith; in 1893 a set of five panels depicting the fairies from *A Midsummer Night's Dream*, embroidered by Una Taylor; in 1899 'St George and the Dragon', worked by Sophie Heywood; and in 1903 'The Woodside', worked by Mrs Ward. One printed and four woven textiles are in the V&A.

Taylor, Edward Ingram (d.1923) Artist. He exhibited two textile designs – for a carpet, 'Waterbabies', in 1899, and for an appliqué and embroidered panel in 1903.

Taylor, Una Artevelde (active by 1888) Embroideress. Little is known of her training and early life. It is probable that she was Irish, as she was first mentioned in the Arts and Crafts Exhibitions as the designer of embroidered picture frames worked by the Donegal Industrial Fund. She also embroidered an Irish National Banner exhibited in 1890. She was an excellent embroideress who used designs by many leading artists and designers, among them W. B. Richmond, E. H. Stephens, J. D. Batten, Graham Robertson, Philip

Burne-Jones, Heywood Sumner and Walter Crane. She exhibited embroideries from 1888 until 1910 but continued to work long afterwards. She was a close friend of May Morris and a fellow member of the Women's Guild of Art.

Taylor, Walter (active from the 1890s) Designer and weaver. He joined Morris & Co. as an apprentice tapestry weaver at the age of fourteen and became one of the firm's most experienced hands. He left some time after 1905 to qualify as a teacher and, eventually, became Head of the Weaving Department at the Central School of Arts and Crafts. He exhibited three designs for tapestry in 1906, including a preparatory study for a kingfisher in 'Love and the Pilgrim', a tapestry woven by Morris & Co. with figures designed by Burne-Jones.

Templeton & Co. (also known as James Templeton and J. & J. S. Templeton) Carpet manufacturers, established in Glasgow in 1839. At first they wove chenille carpets by a patented process; by 1855 they also produced machine-woven Axminster and Brussels carpets. For a short period from the late 1870s until 1886 they manufactured machine-woven *portières*. In 1888 they opened a new factory in Crown Street, Glasgow, built in a polychrome Venetian style, which was nicknamed 'The Doge's Palace'. A foremost manufacturer of artistic carpeting in the 1880s, Templeton's bought patterns from many of the leading designers of the day including Voysey, Day, Crane, J. S. Rigby, Cecil Millar and the Silver Studio. Through Alexander Millar, Artistic Director in the 1890s, the firm became actively involved in local education. They were particularly interested in the work of the Glasgow School of Art, employing a number of ex-students. Templeton's were one of the first manufacturers to exhibit, showing Axminster carpets designed by J. A. Heaton in 1888, and a Brussels carpet designed by Crane in 119 1903. The V&A owns two Brussels carpets made from designs by Crane.

Tomkinson and Adam Carpet manufacturers established in 148 Kidderminster in 1869 by William Adam, a carpet weaver, and Michael Tomkinson, a yarn agent. At first the firm produced chenille rugs, having bought Brinton's plant; from 1878 they specialized in the manufacture of machine-woven Axminster carpets. In the late nineteenth century they bought designs from British and foreign studios and freelance designers, among them Haité, Butterfield, Voysey and the Silver Studio. Voysey, who was under contract to produce ten designs a year, provided their most popular patterns and continued to sell to the firm until the 1930s. They

showed a portion of carpet at the 1895 Manchester Arts and
50 Crafts Exhibition, and Voysey designs (from their 'Aluto'
range) in the 1896 and 1899 Arts and Crafts Exhibitions.
The V&A owns two examples similar to those exhibited in
London (one of the 'Wykehamist' design) and a complete
71 carpet bought from Liberty's.

Townsend, Charles Harrison (1851–1928) Architect and
designer, best known for his two finest buildings, the
Whitechapel Art Gallery and the Horniman Museum. He
produced only a few textile designs, although one of his
favourite architectural decorative schemes, of rows of
lollipop-shaped, flat-leaved trees, is echoed in repeating
textiles and appliqué embroideries by others. In 1892 he
supplied some large-scale designs to Alexander Morton and
it is also likely that he sold patterns to A. H. Lee. He exhibited architectural drawings and other designs but no textiles
are recorded. The V&A possesses one design, 'Omar', and
two woven samples of this in different colourways.

Townsend, W. G. Paulson (1868–1941) Embroidery
designer and writer. In 1899 he published the influential
Embroidery or The Craft of the Needle (with a preface by
Walter Crane). Covering both historical sources and technique, the book illustrates many of his own pieces. He
designed embroideries which were worked at the Royal
School of Art Needlework, including a new town standard
for Preston, finished in 1903, when he was Art Director of
the school. He was a member of the Society of Designers and
his 1900 lecture to them entitled 'Design for Embroidery' was
published in *The Artist*. He was a well respected critic and
examiner for embroidery organizations, such as the Society
of Certificated Embroideresses (later to become the
Embroiderers' Guild). He wrote magazine articles and in
January 1902 he became the editor of the first issue of the *Art
Workers' Quarterly* which, amongst other features, published
scale designs for embroidery. The V&A owns several textile
designs.

Traquair, Phoebe Ann (1852–1936) Painter, calligrapher,
bookbinder, embroideress, metalworker and designer. She
trained at Dublin School of Art and moved to Edinburgh
when in 1872 she married Ramsay Traquair, Keeper of
Natural History of the Royal Scottish Museum. Much of her
large-scale needlework was done in association with the
Scottish architect Sir Robert Lorimer, although she

148. The Axminster
looms at **Tomkinson and
Adam**, Kidderminster,
c. 1899.

149. Cotton, roller-printed on a woven figured ground by **Turnbull and Stockdale**, probably manufactured for Liberty's, c.1900.

designed and worked most of her embroideries alone. Her finest set are four allegorical panels inspired by the account of
75,76 Denys d'Auzerrois in Walter Pater's *Imaginary Portraits*. Embroidered between 1895 and 1902 and exhibited in 1903, they show her skills not only as a draughtsman but also as a technician, the ground being completely covered with stitches. The V&A has designs and a small collection of her domestic embroideries, including a matching tablecloth and tea cosy worked partially in chenille.

† **Turnbull and Stockdale** Printed fabric manufacturers. In 1881 William Turnbull, a textile printer, started the Rosebank Print Works in an early nineteenth-century woollen mill at Stubbins in Lancashire. From the beginning he used block- and roller-printing. By 1883 he employed twelve men. In that year he went into partnership with a mathematician, William Stockdale, whose skills as a chemist and mechanic were matched only by his business acumen. Turnbull had had the insight in 1881 to engage Lewis F. Day as Artistic Director. Day worked with great enthusiasm and not only provided a great many of his own designs but through his contacts in the trade and fashionable London

helped to make the firm one of the leading printers of the period. In 1891 Turnbull's employed fifty-eight people and also undertook bleaching and dyeing both at Rosebank and at their second factory nearby, the Irwell Print Works, Stacksteads, which they had taken some time before 1888. In the 1880s a number of indigo-discharge prints were produced and Turnbull's became noted for their reversible 'duplex' printed cloths. They were contract printers to such London shops as Liberty's, Maple's and Goodyer's and were also represented in most large provincial cities under their own name. In Glasgow their agent was Stevenson of Union Street, and in London, William Bennett at 10 Oxford Circus Avenue. They took part in many Arts and Crafts Exhibitions, including the first, in 1888, and continued to participate in the twentieth century. They also exhibited widely elsewhere, for instance at the 1890 and 1895 Manchester Arts and Crafts Exhibitions. The V&A owns a collection of designs, printed cottons and velveteens produced between the late 1880s and 1910. Although most of the textiles were designed by Day, there are also patterns by Voysey, Butterfield, Mawson, Harry Napper and Alfred Carpenter.

Vallance, Aymer (1862–1943) Writer and designer, educated at Oriel College, Oxford. He lectured on Gothic architecture to the Architectural Association and medieval ecclesiastical art remained his greatest artistic source. He was a close friend of William Morris and wrote (with his approval) an extensive biography covering Morris's artistic achievements. He contributed many articles on contemporary artists and designers and reviews to the *Art Journal* and *The Studio*. Although little is known about his own work he produced patterns for woven textiles and designs for embroideries, mostly for the church. Between 1893 and 1903 twelve embroideries designed by him were displayed, among them a number worked by Bessie Huggett and her

150

150. Aymer **Vallance**: design in Indian ink and Chinese white for a silk damask, c. 1890-1900.

pupils. In 1896 two silk damasks designed by him were exhibited by the Spitalfields Silk Association. In 1900 Miss Huggett also worked with him on a banner for St Stephen's Church, Lewisham. The V&A owns one design.

Vigers, Allan Francis (1858–1921) Architect, illuminator, and designer of wallpapers, embroidery and textiles. Best known for his wallpapers, he produced textile designs for G. P. & J. Baker, Warner & Sons and Alexander Morton. 41 His minutely detailed naturalistic floral patterns, usually on white ground, are instantly recognizable and his style 'spells disaster to the plagiarist' (*Art Workers' Quarterly*, 1902). In 1896, 1903 and 1916 he exhibited designs for embroideries and printed and woven textiles, as well as an embroidered cushion. G. P. & J. Baker showed examples of his 'Rose' 27 design in printed linen and silk in 1903 and a similar design in silk in 1916. The V&A owns a number of designs and one printed linen.

Vigers, Frederick (active from *c.* 1895) Designer of wallpapers, furniture and textiles. In 1895 he showed a 'painted tapestry' at the Manchester Arts and Crafts Exhibition. A silk woven by Warner & Sons from his design called 'St Louis' was made into an altar frontal and displayed at the St Louis Exhibition of 1904. From 1907 he concentrated on designing reproductions for printed furnishings, woven fabrics and canvas work embroideries, of which several were published in the *Studio Year Book* between 1908 and 1915. He was described in the 1911 issue as 'one of the most versatile of our designers'. He showed an embroidered altar cloth in 1906, and a piece of lace and a hanging, 'Apollo and Daphne', in 1910. The V&A owns three designs.

Voysey, Charles Francis Annesley (1857–1941) Architect † and designer of all forms of decorative art, one of the most original and influential in the late nineteenth and twentieth centuries. He studied architecture under J. P. Seddon, Saxon Snell and George Devey, and in 1882 set up his own practice. On the advice of his friend A. H. Mackmurdo, he produced wallpaper designs while waiting for architectural commissions and, from the late 1880s onwards, drew an enormous number of repeating designs for wallpapers, woven and printed textiles and carpets. He sold these to such manufacturers as A. H. Lee, J. W. & C. Ward, Alexander Morton, Morton Sundour, G. P. & J. Baker, Stead McAlpin, Thomas Wardle, Turnbull and Stockdale, Donald Brothers, Foxton's, Templeton's and Tomkinson and Adam and to the shops Liberty's, Wylie and Lochhead, and Story's. He was a shrewd businessman, under contract to both Alex-

151. C. F. A. **Voysey**: 'The House that Jack Built', watercolour design for a nursery furnishing, dated 1929. When Morton Sundour produced the printed fabric the rats were left out of the pattern.

ander Morton and Tomkinson's to provide a certain number of designs every year. Existing patterns reveal that he never wasted ideas, as he continually updated and transposed them from one technique to another. One pattern produced as a printed textile in the early 1890s reappeared in the late 1920s as a carpet design. He understood textile techniques, however, and often wrote technical instructions on his designs. The development of his style can be followed quite closely in his textile designs. Of his patterns the earliest, drawn in the late 1880s, consist of traditional repeats based on historic forms, but by the mid–1890s his work was dominated by flowing patterns incorporating pastel-coloured birds, animals, hearts, flowers and trees in silhouette. These are his most characteristic and original designs. From about 1910 onwards, the motifs are dispersed and his patterns show a preference for narrative themes, many made for the nursery. Voysey's work was well known on the Continent; although it was popular with French Art Nouveau designers, his influence was felt more dramatically by the founders of the Modern Movement. Designs and fabrics exhibited in 1888, 1889, 1896, and 1903 included textiles and carpets made by Alexander Morton and Tomkinson and Adam and embroideries worked by Annie Reynolds-Stephens. The V&A owns an extensive collection of designs, woven and printed fabrics and machine-woven and hand-knotted carpets.

Walton, George (1867–1933) Architect and designer. He had no formal architectural training but left school early, became a bank clerk and attended evening classes at Glasgow School of Art. In 1888 he started his own interior decoration and design firm, George Walton & Co., and decorated and furnished several houses in the Glasgow area between 1889 and 1896. In 1898 he moved to London and by the end of the century had shops in Glasgow, London and York. He was much admired on the Continent, promoted there (like Mackintosh and Baillie Scott) by Hermann Muthesius in his influential book *Das Englische Haus* (1904– 5). Most of Walton's textile designs have special relevance to his interiors, like the stencilled linens which he used as wall hangings in a house at Brasted in Kent. His woven 47 textiles and carpets were produced by Alexander Morton. Although George Walton & Co. exhibited in 1890, his first textile, a woven silk and linen fabric, was not shown until 1899. A stencilled linen followed in 1906 and woven carpets 86 by Alexander Morton in 1910. Mrs George Walton exhibited a child's woven 'and ornamented' coat in 1903. The firm also showed stencilled linens and silk and linen fabrics

WARDLE ART FABRICS.

DEBENHAM & FREEBODY *invite attention to the* Art Decorative Fabrics *of* MR. THOMAS WARDLE, *in*

HAND-PRINTED VELVETS.

CRETONNES.   CURTAIN MATERIALS.

Indian Corah and Tussore Silks.

AND TO A VARIETY OF

FABRICS IN SILK, WOOLLEN, COTTON & LINEN.

PLAIN, PRINTED, AND DYED FOR DRESSES.

HOUSEHOLD ✦ & ✦ CHURCH ✦ DECORATION.

IN PERMANENT COLOURS.

152. Debenham and Freebody advertisement for **Wardle** fabrics, published in 1888. In that year Wardle closed his own London shop, and the stock may have come directly from there.

in room settings at the Glasgow Exhibition of 1901. The V&A has a sample of stencilled linen and a carpet from Brasted; a silk and linen fabric which was used in Elm Bank House, York, and Rowntree's Tea Rooms in Scarborough; and designs made for Morton's.

† **Wardle, Thomas** (1831–1909) Silk dyer and printer. The son of Joshua Wardle, a silk dyer, he entered his father's business after school. By 1880 he owned two print works at Leek, the Churnet Works, used for commercial dyeing and printing, and the Hencroft Works, where he concentrated on experimental work. From the early 1870s he had been fascinated both by the production of silk and by its dyeing and printing. By 1880 he had successfully dyed tusser silk and made a modest attempt at sericulture. He was a founder member of the Silk Association and for many years its President. He lectured extensively on the subject. From 1875 he worked with William Morris at the Hencroft Works, reviving recipes for vegetable dyes, and Morris entrusted him with the printing of fourteen of his designs which Wardle continued to manufacture well into the twentieth century. Wardle was very interested in Eastern patterns and travelled a great deal collecting ideas. He imported silks from

India which he dyed and over-printed in Leek, often selling them through Liberty's. Printed silks, wool, challis, cottons and velveteens were dyed with both vegetable and synthetic dyes, described as being 'in artistic and permanent colours'. Wardle bought work from many leading designers – Day, Crane, Butterfield, Voysey, Sidney Mawson, E. G. Reuter, Léon Solon, Joseph Doran and Cecil Millar. His son, Thomas Wardle, Jr, also provided designs, including eight which were shown in 1889, 1890 and 1893. In the 1870s Thomas Wardle also undertook the dyeing of yarns for Morris & Co.'s embroidery and carpet weaving. He produced all the embroidery silks and printed silk and cotton ground fabrics for the Leek Embroidery Society, which was directed by his wife. Wardle sold most of his textiles through shops such as Liberty's, Story's, Howard & Sons and Heal's. Between 1883 and 1888, however, he also maintained a shop himself, Wardle & Co., in New Bond Street, in partnership with W. S. Brough. Wardle was an enthusiastic early Committee member of the Arts and Crafts Society, and exhibited frequently. He also took part in both the 1890 and 1895 Manchester Arts and Crafts Exhibitions. The V&A has a wide range of prints, a pattern book, and some raw silk given by Wardle.

Warner & Sons Silk weavers, trading under this name from 1891, founded by Benjamin Warner (1828–1908), a silk designer and weaver who trained at the Spitalfields School of Design. In 1867 he went into his first partnership, with William Folliott. His firm was known as Warner, Sillett & Ramm (1870–75), Warner & Ramm (1875–90), Warner, Ramm & Stanway (1878–July 1879) and Warner & Sons. It also took over the goodwill, plant and designs of various other companies including Charles Norris (in 1885) and Daniel Walters & Sons (in 1894). Warner's first workshop was in Spitalfields, but in 1873 larger premises were taken at Hollybush Gardens, Bethnal Green. In 1895 the whole weaving operation was moved to Walters's New Mill factory at Braintree in Essex. Warner's have always been noted for high technical achievement and did not adopt power-loom weaving until 1919. As well as a large traditional range of floral patterns, they bought designs from many free-lance designers, among them Butterfield, Crane, the Silver Studio, Cecil Millar, Frederick Vigers, Sidney Mawson and G. Randall Kennerley. They also continued to produce the most avant-garde designs of the firms they had taken over, by notable figures such as Owen Jones and Bruce Talbert. Two of Benjamin Warner's sons, Frank and Alfred, became partners. On his father's death, Frank took over management of the factory and hand weaving of silk and his older brother, Alfred, looked after printed fabrics, which had been stocked since 1886. Warner's did not become printers until they acquired a factory in Dartford in the 1920s. Warner & Sons exhibited two textiles, a woven woollen 'tapestry' designed by Cecil Millar in 1903 and a silk damask, 'Birds and Baskets', by Rex Silver, in 1916. The V&A owns designs and silks dating from the 1870s onwards, and in 1970 held an exhibition, *A Century of Warner Fabrics 1870–1970*.

Webb, Philip (1831–1915) Architect and designer. In 1854 he joined G. E. Street's office where he met William Morris, who became a close friend. Webb ran his own practice from *c.* 1859 and designed the Red House for William and Jane Morris in 1859–60. As a founder member of Morris, Marshall, Faulkner & Co. in 1861 he helped to design early church furnishings made by the firm. He also provided drawings of animals and birds for early Morris printed textiles 37 and for 'The Forest' tapestry, exhibited in 1888 and 1890. He designed several embroideries which were worked privately by May Morris, including a superfrontal made for the Rochester and Southwark Deaconess House in 1898–9. In 1916 May Morris exhibited a sideboard cloth which she had embroidered from his design. The superfrontal and Webb's design for it are both now in the V&A.

Willcock, Arthur (active from the 1890s) Wallpaper and textile designer. His name is little known, although he was 153 talented and versatile and his printed cottons display highly attractive and original patterns. Some of these are illustrated in an article about his designs in the Proceedings of the Society of Designers (*The Artist*, 1900). He sold designs to British and foreign manufacturers and to shops including Liberty's, John Burnet and Sons, Story's, Newman, Smith and Newman, Franklin and Franklin, and Joseph and Edward Buckley of Manchester. One design sold to Gros Roman of Mulhouse (Textile Museum, Mulhouse), is dated 15 July 1898. Willcock exhibited three textile designs in 1889 and one in 1899. The V&A own several original designs.

Willshaw, Arthur (active from *c.* 1875) Designer of silk and wool textiles, many of which were made by J. W. & C. Ward of Halifax and sold through Liberty's at the end of the nineteenth century. These are illustrated in 'English-made Textiles' (Proceedings of the Society of Designers, *The Artist*, 1899). One fabric is now in the Museum at Trondheim in Norway.

Wilson, John, & Sons Retailers in Bond Street founded in the early nineteenth century. Listed as 'household linen

153. Arthur **Willcock**: printed cotton manufactured by Newman, Smith and Newman, c. 1900.

warehousemen', the firm specialized in the sale of linen damasks. At the end of the century they also sold window hangings of lace and Madras muslin, as well as supplying stencilled linens. They commissioned damask designs from Day, Dresser, Robert Anning Bell and Walter Crane (who supplied their most popular pattern, 'The Senses', and a set 68 of d'oyleys showing 'Flora's Retinue'). Most of the damasks were woven for Wilson's by Irish weavers, including Ireland Brothers & Co. of Belfast. In 1899 the firm became 'John Wilson's Successors Ltd' and *c.* 1903 they moved their shop to 188 Regent Street.

Wright, Ellen Mary (active from *c.* 1890) Embroideress and designer. She joined Morris & Co. from school *c.* 1890 and was trained by May Morris. She completed numerous embroideries for the firm, including hangings exhibited in 1890, 1893 and 1899. By 1905 she was teaching embroidery at Camberwell School of Art and her students' work was exhibited in 1906. In 1912 and 1916 she showed embroideries designed by herself and her sister Fanny Isobel Wright, who also worked as an embroideress for Morris & Co. and taught at Camberwell School of Art until her marriage.

Notes

Abbreviations
A & C papers = Arts and Crafts Exhibition Society papers, given to the Victoria and Albert Museum by the Society of Designer Craftsmen and now housed at the Archive of Art and Design, Blythe Road
PRO = Public Record Office, Kew
V&A = Victoria and Albert Museum

Introduction
p. 9 1. None of the recommendations of the 1863 Royal Commission set up to look into the Royal Academy had been acted upon.
2. The Academy offered neither season tickets nor exhibition catalogues to the press.
10 3. These included W. R. Lethaby, Gerald Horsley, Mervyn Macartney, Ernest Newton and E. S. Prior.
4. Quoted in Gillian Naylor, *The Arts and Crafts Movement*, 1971, p. 120.
5. Other members were G. T. Robinson, James D. Linton, E. F. Brentall, Sacheverell Coke, H. Arthur Kennedy and George Simons, with H. M. Paget, Henry Page, T. Erat Harrison and J. T. Nettleship joining later.
6. Walter Crane, *An Artist's Reminiscences*, 1907, p. 224.
7. ibid., p. 223.
8. Quoted by Gavin Stamp in 'A Hundred Years of the Art Workers' Guild', in *Beauty Awakening*, exhibition catalogue, Brighton, 1984.
11 9. Walter Crane, 'The Arts and Crafts', *Murray's Magazine*, November 1889, p. 651.
10. Quoted from *The Artist and Journal of Home Culture*, VII, 1886, p. 301.
11. 'Programme for a National Art Exhibition', *The British Architect*, XXVI, 17 September 1886, p. 277.
12. A & C papers.
13. ibid. (Agenda to the second meeting of the Provisional Committee, 19 February 1887).
14. Another important offshoot of this organization was the Association for the Advancement of Art and its Application to Industry, which held three yearly congresses in Liverpool (1888), Edinburgh (1889) and Birmingham (1890). Because of the interesting composition of its membership and the subjects chosen for discussion the Association became one of the most significant forums of the period.
15. A. H. Mackmurdo, *History of the Arts and Crafts Movement*, hand- and typewritten manuscript, William Morris Gallery, Walthamstow.
12 16. A & C papers. The collection, initiated by Benson, includes a short account of the foundation of the Society by him.

14 17. J. Scarratt Rigby, 'Remarks on Morris Work and its influence on British Decorative Arts of Today', *Art Workers' Quarterly*, I, 1902, pp. 2-5 and 61-4.
18. Quoted in Edward G. Gregory, 'English Village Arts', *House and Garden*, IV, 1903, p. 62.
19. *The Artist*, XXVIII, 1900, p. 145.
15 20. *The House*, V, July 1899, p. 162.
21. A & C papers.
22. The Committee Meeting of 7 January 1888 proposed that twenty-five selected members should be asked to contribute £10 each. On the whole the collection was successful, with some paying more and some less.
23. Three alternative financial arrangements had been discussed: the Gallery would receive a flat rent of £500, a rent of £400 plus half of the profits, or, as was decided upon, a rent of £300 plus two-thirds of the profits.
24. A. H. Mackmurdo, op. cit.

1. The Artistic and Industrial Background
25 1. The exhibition had a far more direct effect on the manufacturers of the cottons exhibited, who created a public outcry fearing that their businesses would suffer from being singled out for criticism in what they considered an unfair way.
26 2. *Plans, Elevations, Sections and Details of the Alhambra* (1842).
3. In the archive of Warner & Sons, Braintree.
4. First published as a series of articles in Cassel's *Technical Educator* from 1870.
5. From £3,343,761 to £5,908,629. Details given by Thomas Wardle in 'Notes on the Collection of Silks exhibited under the auspices of the Ladies' National Silk Association', in the catalogue of the Manchester Arts and Crafts Exhibition, 1895.

2. The Evolution of a Style
31 1. Examples of these silks now in the V&A were given by Wardle following their display in the British India Pavilion at the Paris Exhibition of 1878.
2. This textile was purchased by the Indian Section of the V&A in 1880. See *Liberty's 1875-1975*, exhibition catalogue, V&A, 1975.
34 3. Dresser had himself attended the School of Design at Somerset House.
36 4. See *From East to West: Textiles from G. P. & J. Baker*, exhibition catalogue, V&A, 1984.
42 5. Lille weavers and Alsatian printers were particularly interested in British work, and one manufacturer, Gros Roman of Mulhouse, who had been represented in London since 1882, bought a great variety of British designs to use as printed textiles.
6. See Registration of Designs, PRO. The

colouring and eccentric patterns of some of the textiles printed by Steiner's between 1899 and 1907, now in the V&A, show clearly that they were not made for the home market.
7. Mackintosh produced a great number of patterns for Foxton's and Sefton's in his later career.
45 8. The border design had been registered much earlier: No. 389703, 9 November 1882. Registration of Designs, PRO.
48 9. Aymer Vallance, 'The Progress of the Industrial Arts. No. 6. Velvets, Velveteens and Plushes', *Art Journal*, 1891, p. 234.
49 10. Three examples are in the V&A.
11. Lucie H. Armstrong, 'Silks and Satins', *Art Journal*, 1891, p. 19.
12. Prof. Robert Beaumont, 'Szczepanik's Inventions for Textile Designs', *The Furnisher*, December 1899, pp. 83-6.
13. 'The Jacquard Loom Improved', *The Furnisher*, November 1899, p. xxxii.
14. Published as 'Decoration and Furnishing', *The Artist and Journal of Home Culture*, 1 August 1885, pp. 237-9.
15. 'The Furnishing and Decoration of the House, No. V, Carpets and Curtains', *Art Journal*, 1892, p. 311.
16. One commentator suggested that the only good use for power-loom-woven fabrics was to be cut up for upholstery: R. Jervis, 'Woven Wall Hangings', *Arts and Crafts*, III, 1905, p. 178.
17. 'The English Revival of Decorative Arts', *Fortnightly Review*, LII, no. 312, 1 December 1891, p. 31.
50 18. 'The Arts and Crafts Exhibition – II', *Magazine of Art*, XX, November 1896– April 1897, p. 63.
53 19. 'Stencilling in House Decoration', *Magazine of Art*, XXI, May–October 1897, pp. 161-3.
20. 'Stencil Decoration', *Magazine of Art*, XXII, November 1897, pp. 45-6.
54 21. F. Hargreaves Smith, 'The Dyeing of Fabric', *The Artist and Journal of Home Culture*, XXIII, September 1898, pp. 31-3.
22. 'Stencilled Fabrics for Curtains and Furniture Coverings', *The Artist and Journal of Home Culture*, XXII, November 1897, pp. 183-4.
23. 'First International *Studio* Exhibition Part II', *The Studio*, XXIV, January 1902, p. 248.
24. 'Recent Examples of English Decoration', *The Craftsman*, VI, 1904, pp. 97-108.

3. Textiles in the Arts and Crafts Exhibitions
65 1. *Furniture and Decoration*, 16 November 1896, p. 167.
2. Stated by William Morris in an interview with Aymer Vallance, 'The Revival of Tapestry Weaving', *The Studio*, III, July 1894, p. 101.

66 3. In 1888, 1889, 1890, 1893, 1896, 1899, 1903, 1906, 1910, 1912 and 1916.

4. Consisting of William Morris, Lewis F. Day, Mervyn Macartney, Heywood Sumner, Stephen Webb, W. A. S. Benson, the President (Walter Crane) and the Secretary (Ernest Radford).

5. As late as 1893 the Selection Committee had to write to Liberty's, Maison Helbronner and Robinson & Co. telling them that they could not automatically expect to be included without first going through the selection procedure; and in the same year J. Aldam Heaton threatened to withdraw his guarantee from the Society if not granted space.

6. Wardle withdrew two 'designs' after a Mr Rigby said that they were his work. To defend himself Wardle showed the Committee a lithograph from a French magazine which he argued disproved one claim by Rigby and said that the other design was based on a Persian tile. A & C papers.

7. Art Journal, 1888, p. 349.

68 8. See Catalogue of A. H. Mackmurdo and the Century Guild Collection, William Morris Gallery, Walthamstow. Individual members of the Guild continued to exhibit separately, with 'Mackmurdo and Horne' showing a screen in 1889, and Selwyn Image designing a number of embroideries for the Royal School of Art Needlework, the Decorative Needlework Society and various individuals between 1889 and 1906.

9. The accounts for the first exhibition showed a profit of £149.16s.2d. after expenses put at £1,082.12s.1d. (which included rent at £300 and fittings for the exhibition costing £24.12s.4d.). The profits were split with the New Gallery as agreed and £53.2s.1d. was retained by the Society.

10. Morris had originally believed that the aims of the Society were unrealistic and pointless and that it would do nothing to rectify the injustices caused by class division and a search after profits by most manufacturers. See J. W. Mackail, The Life of William Morris, 1899, ch. XVIII.

11. Mrs. Ashbee's piano cover, designed by her son, C. R. Ashbee, is in the V&A.

70 12. Illustrated London News, 12 October 1889, p. 462.

13. Mary Buckle embroidered a great many of Day's designs and in 1901 the two published the embroidery manual Art in Needlework.

14. The figure was 18,785 for the full period of the exhibition. Attendances were not always a measure of success, however: in 1893, one of the most successful years, the figure was 14,140.

15. Admission cost 1s. in 1888. A season ticket was available for 5s.

16. Textile lectures (which were all published in the catalogue) were 'Textiles' by William Morris (1888), 'Of Dyeing as an Art' by William Morris, 'Of Embroidery' by May Morris, and 'Of Lace' by Alan S. Cole (1889), and a set of five lectures on embroidery given by May Morris, Mary M. Turner, Alan S. Cole and Selwyn Image (1890).

71 17. On receiving his guaranteed sum back, J. Hungerford Pollen exclaimed, 'I gaze on the cheque as something so phenomenal that I conclude such a return must be without precedent.' A & C papers.

18. The three designs, which include 'The Four Seasons' by Crane, were all registered on the same day in December 1893. See Registration of Designs, PRO.

19. Art Journal, 1895, pp. 286-7.

20. The Studio, IX, October 1896, p. 54.

21. Lewis F. Day, 'Fifth Exhibition of the Arts and Crafts', Art Journal, 1896, p. 329.

76 22. Rowat was Jessie Newbery's maiden name, so these embroideresses are likely to have been related to her.

23. In 1895-6 the Committee received requests from Paris, Brussels and Rotterdam, as well as Dublin.

24. Magazine of Art, XX, November 1896, p. 32.

78 25. The regulations in force in 1899 stated that textiles and needlework had to be either arranged as hangings or shown in frames and that framed pieces of printed, woven, stamped or other manufactured materials must be shown in single widths one yard (90 cm) in length. See The House, V, May 1899, pp. 94-5.

26. The canvas was supplied by Burnet & Co. of Regent Street at a cost of £16 and the trees by C. W. Buck of Covent Garden at 10s. a week plus £2 for delivery and maintenance. A & C papers.

89 27. In that year the New Gallery had suggested that the Society share the premises with the Society of Designers.

28. Originally designed as a restaurant, the New Gallery was returned to this use directly after the 1910 Exhibition.

29. The Studio, XXXVII, 1906, pp. 50-51.

30. The Artist, XXVIII, 1900, p. 148.

4. Designers, Manufacturers and Shops

95 1. Of these 8,172 were entered into the competition; 1,206 received awards, including 14 gold medals. See The Artist, XXIX, September–December 1900, p. 74.

2. J. Scarratt Rigby, 'Central School of Arts and Crafts: Exhibition of Students' Work', Art Workers' Quarterly, I, 1902, pp. 149-52.

96 3. The Silver Studio sold the 'Silvern Series' of photographs of objects from the V&A which were used as source material for designs.

4. Art Journal, 1908, p. 19.

5. See Frederick Dolman, 'The Quaint and Grotesque in Cotton Designing', Magazine of Art, XXIII, November 1898, pp. 34-7. The atelier of Joseph Waterhouse showed at the 1895 Manchester Arts and Crafts Exhibition and the catalogue lists some of the designers.

6. A. F. P., 'The Work of Beatrice A. Waldram', Arts and Crafts, IV, 1905-6, pp. 75-80.

97 7. Surprisingly, Dresser's two sons were apprenticed to the Silver Studio and did not train under their father.

8. 'Art and Handicraft', Magazine of Art, XI, October 1888, p. 410.

98 9. In the 1903 Arts and Crafts Exhibition Day's entries were labelled 'designed for the most part to meet the conditions of practical manufacture', which many saw as personal criticism of their work.

10. Art Journal, 1896, p. 330.

101 11. Some Voysey designs with their signatures rubbed out have recently been found by the staff of the Silver Studio Collection at the Middlesex Polytechnic. Harry Napper continued to sell designs through the Silver Studio after he left to work on his own in 1898.

102 12. 'Designers' Jottings', The Artist, XXIV, 1899, p. 213.

13. A. H. Lee on 11 February 1889, no. 119460; G. P. & J. Baker on 28 March 1893, no. 209883. Registration of Designs, PRO. Although Lee is listed as a 'tapestry manufacturer' his first registration is inexplicably represented by a printed cotton.

14. Liberty registered in both his own name and that of his shop.

103 15. A & C papers.

113 16. See Heal & Son pattern books in the Archive of Art and Design of the V&A, Blythe Road.

114 17. 'The First International Studio Exhibition Part II', The Studio, XXIV, 1901-2. p. 245.

18. The V&A owns a small crewelwork panel which was copied from an Ellen Welby design published in Arts and Crafts for June 1904.

19. This is now in the Rachel Kay-Shuttleworth Collection at the National Trust property, Gawthorpe Hall, near Burnley in Lancashire.

20. A number were registered by Thomas Wardle.

116 21. Unfinished kits from Helbronner, Liberty's and Morris & Co. are in the V&A.

Bibliography

Books

Adburgham, Alison, *Liberty's: A Biography of a Shop*, 1975

Anscombe, Isabelle, and Charlotte Gere, *Arts and Crafts in Britain and America*, 1978

Benjamin, Frederick A., *The Ruskin Linen Industry of Keswick*, 1974

Billcliffe, Roger, *Mackintosh Textiles*, 1982

Callen, Anthea, *Angel in the Studio: Women of the Arts and Crafts Movement 1870-1914*, 1979

Cooper, Jeremy, *Victorian and Edwardian Furniture and Interiors*, 1987

Cooper, Nicholas, *The Opulent Eye*, 1976

Durrant, Stuart, *Ornament*, 1986

Goodden, Susanna, *At the Sign of the Fourposter: A Story of Heal's*, 1984

Howard, Constance, *Twentieth Century Embroidery in Great Britain to 1939*, 1981

Johnson, Alan, and Kevin Moore, *The Tapestry Makers*, Merseyside Docklands Community History Project, 1986

King, Donald, ed., *British Textile Designs in the Victoria and Albert Museum*, III, Victorian to Modern, 1980

Marsh, Jan, *Jane and May Morris*, 1986

Morris, Barbara, *Victorian Embroidery*, 1962

— *Inspiration for Design*, 1986

Morton, Jocelyn, *Three Generations in a Family Textile Firm*, 1971

Naylor, Gillian, *The Arts and Crafts Movement*, 1971

Oman, Charles C., and Jean Hamilton, *Wallpapers*, 1982

Parry, Linda, *William Morris Textiles*, 1983

Prickett, Elizabeth, *Ruskin Lace and Linen Work*, 1985

Richardson, Margaret, *Architects of the Arts and Crafts Movement*, 1983

Rowe, Veronica, *Clare Embroidery*, 1985

Ryecroft, Elizabeth, Unpublished thesis on Lewis F. Day, Royal College of Art, 1980

Service, Alastair, *Edwardian Architecture*, 1977

Spencer, Isobel, *Walter Crane*, 1975

Stansky, Peter, *Redesigning the World: William Morris, the 1880s, and the Arts and Crafts*, 1985

Tattersall, C. E. C., *A History of British Carpets*, 1934

Catalogues

Boston, Museum of Fine Arts: Wendy Kaplan and others, *The Art that is Life*, 1987

Brighton, Royal Pavilion, Art Gallery and Museum: *Beauty Awakening: The Centenary of the Art Workers' Guild 1884-1984*, 1984

— John Brandon-Jones and others, *C. F. A. Voysey: architect and designer 1857-1941*, 1978

Birmingham Museum and Art Gallery: Alan Crawford, ed., *By Hammer and Hand: the Arts and Crafts Movement in Birmingham*, 1984

Glasgow Museum and Art Gallery: *Glasgow School of Art Embroidery 1894-1920*, 1980

London, Middlesex Polytechnic: *A London Design Studio: the Silver Studio Collection*, 1980

— *Art Nouveau Designs from the Silver Studio Collection 1885-1910*, 1986

London, Victoria and Albert Museum: *Victorian and Edwardian Decorative Arts*, 1952

— *A Century of Warner Fabrics 1870-1970*, 1970

— *Victorian Church Art*, 1972

— *The Mortons*, 1973

— *Liberty 1875-1975*, 1975

— Susan Lambert, ed., *Pattern and Design*, 1983

— *From East to West: Textiles from G. P. & J. Baker*, 1984

London, William Morris Gallery, Walthamstow: *Catalogue of A. H. Mackmurdo and the Century Guild Collection*, 1967

Stuttgart, Württembergisches Landesmuseum: Ruth Gronwoldt, *Art-Nouveau-Textil-Dekor Um 1900*, 1980

Warner & Sons: *A Choice of Design 1850-1980*, 1981

Winchester City Museum: *Heywood Sumner: Artist and Archaeologist 1853-1940*, 1986

Illustration Sources

V&A = Victoria and Albert Museum

V&A numbers with the prefix 'E' indicate that the items are part of the collection of the Department of Designs, Prints and Drawings, and those with the prefix 'AAD' are from the Archive of Art and Design of the V&A at Blythe Road. All others can be found in the Department of Textile Furnishings and Dress.

Cover: V&A T.154–1977.
1. V&A T.414–1970.
2. V&A Library – Arts and Crafts Exhibition catalogue.
3. V&A AAD1/20–1980.
4. Liverpool City Libraries.
5. V&A AAD1/5–1980.
6. V&A (Print Room) 7725–1938.
7. V&A E.4199–1915.
8. V&A E.68–1961.
9. G. P. & J. Baker Ltd.
10. V&A Circ.270–1958.
11. V&A T.59–1953.
12. V&A T.10–1953.
13. V&A Circ.99–1966.
14. V&A T.16–1954.
15. V&A T.50–1953.
16. V&A T.57–1953.
17. V&A T.23–1954.
18. Photo: V&A.
19. V&A I.S.53–1881.
20. V&A T.585–1919.
21. V&A Circ.500–1965.
22. National Portrait Gallery.
23. Private Collection.
24. V&A T.91–1973.
25. V&A T.67–1973.
26. V&A T.5–1987.
27. V&A E.5513–1960.
28. V&A T.75–1967.
29. V&A Circ.107–1966.
30. V&A T.280–1965.
31. V&A Circ.253–1966.
32. V&A T.359–1967.
33. Photo: Glasgow Museums and Art Galleries.
34. V&A T.85–1953.
35. V&A Circ.837–1967.
36. Kunstindustrimuseet, Oslo.
37. V&A T.111–1926.
38. V&A T.11–1953.
39. V&A Circ.72–1953.
40. G. P. & J. Baker Ltd.
41. *Studio Yearbook*, 1906, p. 71.
42. *The Studio*, XXVI, 1902, p.99.
43. V&A AAD 2–1978/su 2.
44. V&A AAD 2–1978/su 2.
45. William Morris Gallery, Walthamstow.
46. Chicago Architecture Foundation.
47. *Studio Yearbook*, 1907, p. 117.
48. *The Craftsman*, no. 6, p. 100.
49. National Monuments Record.
50. V&A T.74–1953.
51. National Monuments Record.
52. V&A T.15–1953.
53. V&A Circ.886–1967.
54. V&A E.147–1974.
55. V&A E.148–1974.
56. V&A E.61–1961.
57. V&A T.5–1986.
58. V&A T.173–1978.
59. V&A T.218–1953.
60. V&A T.88–1953.
61. V&A T.84–1953.
62. V&A T.17–1954.
63. William Morris Gallery, Walthamstow.
64. Museum für Kunst und Gewerbe, Hamburg.
65. V&A AAD 8/3–1978.
66. V&A T.31–1923.
67. V&A Circ.239–1966.
68. *Art Journal*, Sept. 1895, p.296.
69. National Museums of Scotland.
70. V&A Circ.95–1966.
71. V&A T.159–1978.
72. V&A T.71 & A–1939.
73. National Monuments Record.
74. Hereford and Worcester County Museum.
75, 76. National Museums of Scotland.
77. *The Studio*, XXV, 1902, p.91.
78. V&A T.127–1953.
79. V&A Circ.206–1964.
80. V&A T.707–1972.
81. Kelmscott Manor, The Society of Antiquaries (photo: A.F. Kersting).
82. V&A T.69–1953.
83. V&A T.68–1953.
84. V&A E.855–1968.
85. V&A T.65–1953.
86. V&A T.65–1946.
87. G. P. & J. Baker Ltd.
88. G. P. & J. Baker Ltd.
89. G. P. & J. Baker Ltd.
90. V&A T.94–1953.
91. G. P. & J. Baker Ltd.
92. Spink & Son Ltd.
93. V&A T.82–1946.
94. V&A Circ.276–1958.
95. V&A Circ.786–1967.
96. V&A T.40–1968.
97. *The Studio*, LXIX, 1917, p.129.
98. Westminster Abbey (photo: V&A).
99. Sotheby's, London.
100. Silver Studio Collection, Middlesex Polytechnic.
101. Nordenfjeldske Kunstindustrimuseum, Trondheim.
102. V&A E.152–1974.
103. V&A T.19–1953.
104. V&A Circ.885–1967.
105. V&A E.245–1954.
106. *The Furnisher*, 1899–1900 (inside front cover).
107. V&A E.1279–1970.
108. V&A T.163–1957.
109. V&A T.180–1957.
110. V&A T.174–1957.
111. V&A T.183–1957.
112. Württembergische Landesmuseum, Stuttgart.
113. V&A T.38–1953.
114. V&A Circ.675–1966.
115. Bellerive Museum, Zurich.
116. Private Collection.
117. V&A T.416–1970.
118. V&A T.415–1970.
119. V&A E.2325–1920.
120. G. P. & J. Baker Ltd.
121. *Art Journal*, Jan. 1905, p.11.
122. National Monuments Record.
123. V&A AAD 2–1978/su 14.
124. William Morris Gallery, Walthamstow.
125. V&A E.69–1961.
126. V&A E.373–1967.
127. H. J. L. J. Massé, *The Art Workers' Guild* (1935).
128. V&A T.111–1953.
129. *Art Workers' Quarterly*, IV, 1905, p.69.
130. National Portrait Gallery.
131. *Art Journal*, Nov. 1906, p.337.
132. Private Collection (photo: V&A).
133. G. P. & J. Baker Ltd.
134. V&A Circ.866–1967.
135. V&A Circ.288–1966.
136. *Art Journal*, Nov. 1897, p.331.
137. V&A T.414–1970.
138. V&A Circ.415–1966.
139. V&A T.369A–1982.
140. V&A T.172–1977.
141. V&A T.253–1982.
142. V&A E.70–1961.
143. Glasgow Museums and Art Galleries.
144. G. P. & J. Baker Ltd.
145. V&A T.774 to D–1972.
146. V&A T.254–1982.
147. V&A T.7–1953.
148. *The Artist*, XXV, 1899, p.201.
149. V&A Circ.273–1958.
150. V&A E.290–1937.
151. V&A E.332–1974.
152. *Catalogue of the Italian Exhibition in London*, 1888.
153. Kunstindustrimuseet, Oslo.

Index

Page numbers in **bold** type indicate a main entry in the Catalogue. Figures in *italic* type refer to illustration numbers and captions.